NIGHT DRIVING

Maxwell,
Love you Son -
Mom

NIGHT DRIVING
Notes from a Prodigal Soul

CHAD BIRD

WILLIAM B. EERDMANS PUBLISHING COMPANY
GRAND RAPIDS, MICHIGAN

Wm. B. Eerdmans Publishing Co.
2140 Oak Industrial Drive NE, Grand Rapids, Michigan 49505
www.eerdmans.com

26 25 24 23 22 21 20 19 18 17   3 4 5 6 7 8 9 10 11 12

ISBN 978-0-8028-7401-6

Library of Congress Cataloging-in-Publication Data

Names: Bird, Chad, author.
Title: Night driving : notes from a prodigal soul / Chad Bird.
Description: Grand Rapids : Eerdmans Publishing Co., 2017. |
    Includes bibliographical references.
Identifiers: LCCN 2017029706 | ISBN 9780802874016 (pbk. : alk. paper)
Subjects: LCSH: Christian life. | Spiritual formation. | Spiritual healing.
Classification: LCC BV4501.3 .B496 2017 | DDC 248.4—dc23
    LC record available at https://lccn.loc.gov/2017029706

Contents

Foreword

L ONG AGO, a handful of German theologians got together and summarized the essentials of the Christian life and faith in a document called the Heidelberg Catechism. It is set in the classic question-and-answer format, and it's famous for the first question and answer:

Q. What is your only comfort in life and in death?

A. That I am not my own, but belong—body and soul, in life and in death—to my faithful Savior, Jesus Christ. He has fully paid for all my sins with his precious blood, and has set me free from the tyranny of the devil. He also watches over me in such a way that not a hair can fall from my head without the will of my Father in heaven; in fact, all things must work together for my salvation. Because I belong to him, Christ, by his Holy Spirit, assures me of eternal life and makes me wholeheartedly willing and ready from now on to live for him.[1]

These words articulate one of great paradoxes of the gospel. It's all about us and our comfort. And it's not about us at all.

It's about us in this sense: "In accordance with what he did and revealed in Jesus Christ," wrote theologian Karl Barth, "God willed from all eternity not to be without man."[2]

The apostle Paul put it this way:

Praise be to the God and Father of our Lord Jesus Christ, who has blessed us in the heavenly realms with every spiritual blessing in Christ. For he chose us in him before the creation of the world to be holy and blameless in his sight. In love he predestined us for adoption to sonship through Jesus Christ, in accordance with his pleasure and will. (Eph. 1:3-5, NIV)

So intent was God on making us family, he would not let human stupidity, weakness, indifference, or even outright rebellion dissuade him from accomplishing "his pleasure and will" toward us. So the gospel is, in one sense, all about our comfort. It's about knowing that because of what Jesus has done for us, we now know God as "Our Father." In explaining these words of the Lord's Prayer, Martin Luther said, "With these words God tenderly invites us to believe that he is our true Father and that we are his true children, so that with all boldness and confidence we may ask him as dear children ask their dear father."[3]

Yet more crucially, the gospel is not about us. That is to say, we have done nothing to bring this extraordinary good news to bear. In fact, we have done a great deal to thwart it, undermine it, and disrupt it. All to no avail, of course. Sinners have a pretty high opinion of their ability to sabotage the purposes of God. God, for his part, just laughs and says, "I'll show *you*." And while we were sinners, he died for us.

And thus the just consequences of sin were meted out. The rebellion that would destroy our relationship with God was itself destroyed. The alienation between God and humankind was healed. As Paul put it, on the cross itself, in the darkest of times when God had seemed to forsake his beloved, "God was reconciling the world to himself in Christ, not counting people's sins against them" (2 Cor. 5:19).

Note the obvious, which for some reason is not as

obvious as it should be: He died for us before we turned from our sins and repented. He reconciled us long before we even realized how estranged we were. "What he has done," wrote Barth, "he has done without us, without the world, without the counsel or help of that which is flesh and lives in the flesh—except only for the flesh of Jesus Christ."[4] It is in this respect that the gospel is not about us and all about what God has done. Our lives—from first to last, in times glorious and hours black and bleak—are not our own but have been and will continue to be in the hands of a good and gracious God.

We like to imagine that we've had something to do with all this: It's the result, at least in part, of our good judgment in receiving the gospel, our commitment to stick with Jesus in the hardest of times, our disciplined spirituality, which includes an accountability partner! To be sure, we say, it is all due to God's grace, but day to day, we're tempted to lean on at least a sliver of effort on our part. It's this sliver that sets us apart from unbelievers and the nominal in faith, isn't it? It's this sliver that makes us worthy of being called children of God. And it's this sliver, however tiny, that we wear like a talisman, like a badge of merit.

Chad Bird, in a theological tradition that began

with the apostle Paul, reminds us that the talisman is an idol. Or better, the sliver is not even that. It's a fantasy to believe we've had anything to do with the grace that God showers upon us. The only difference between us and the common lot of sinners is that we're the sinners who, by God's grace, recognize the truth of our situation: "That I am not my own, but belong—body and soul, in life and in death—to my faithful Savior, Jesus Christ."

As we let that reality sink in—and it takes a lifetime for it to penetrate to the deepest recesses of our souls—we realize there is nothing more comforting. To not be in control means that another, more just and gracious than we can imagine, is.

The way Chad talks about all this will make some readers nervous. The careless reader is going to think that Chad doesn't give a rip about Christian ethics, that he's indifferent to how we live in Christ. Some are going to accuse him of antinomianism—that he believes the law of God is passé, that in light of God's amazing grace, morality is bunk.

When I hear reactions like this to any discussion of grace, it makes me think about the greatest treatise on grace—the book of Romans. In that exposition, Paul has to interrupt his argument repeatedly to answer one particular objection. He is so emphatic about the inconceivable, unmerited nature of grace, his readers naturally exclaim, "What shall we say, then? Shall we go on sinning so that grace may increase?" (Rom. 6:1). And each time Paul repeats, "By no means!" And then he goes on to explain that grace is the only conceivable ground of true Christian ethics.

Chad doesn't deal with this question in this book, but anyone who has read his essays on marriage, on sex, on a number of topics, recognizes that Chad believes what Jesus said about himself, that he did not come to abolish the law but to fulfill it (Matt. 5:17), and that it is the gospel that transforms the human heart to gladly obey Jesus day to day. So Chad would echo Paul in responding "By no means!"

But in this little book, Chad has a singular purpose. He want us to get one thing straight. Before we talk about anything else—especially before we talk about ourselves, what *we* think or do—he wants us to be absolutely clear about what God has done for us in Christ. He wants there to be no mistaking that, even in the darkest of times, we are not our own but belong to another, to one who has our best interests at heart and will never let us go. The more firmly we grasp that, the more we will know a comfort that surpasses human understanding, and then and only then will everything else we are to know and do fall into place.

MARK GALLI
Editor in Chief, *Christianity Today*

CHAPTER ONE

Crouching amidst the Ruins

THERE COMES A TIME in almost everyone's life when they feel like Adam must have felt the first time he watched the sun set. All the beauty and warmth of light morph into night. It doesn't happen instantly. It's not like the flip of a light switch. First there's fear as the sun crawls toward the horizon, then bewilderment as it vanishes, then shock as the world we once knew envelops us with darkness.

In this darkness, we grope about for objects once familiar to us. We look for mementoes of a former life bathed in light. But every direction we pivot, we see our world blanketed by losses we cannot even begin to accept, much less understand. We're paralyzed, crouching amidst the ruins of the life we once had. And we fear the rays of hope will never reappear.

Maybe you've been there. Maybe you're there right

now, in that place void of light. Ten years ago, I watched that sun vanish below the horizon. I felt the bite of fear, the bewilderment, the shock. Then I fell face-first into a world of darkness.

I'm going to tell you my story. I'm inviting you into it. But I'm also inviting you to tell your story alongside mine. To compare narratives of loss, regret, addiction, pain. To compare scars. More importantly, I want us to see our stories in the context of a bigger story. And to see it all as part of a long storyline about ultimate, liberating redemption. Be patient—we'll get there. But we can't move forward until we look at the moments that led us here. So let's begin as the sun sets.

I WAS BUSY LIVING OUT MY DREAMS when all of them came untrue. Those dreams had their genesis in the mid-1990s. Fresh out of college in Texas, I had enrolled in a seminary in Indiana to study for the pastoral ministry. I was twenty-two years old, married, and eager to take on the world for God. My wife and I enjoyed our newlywed years in a small apartment not far from campus.

The life of a student, it turned out, was the life for me. Each day was a veritable feast of theology. I relished the back-and-forth discussions with my classmates. I ordered my life around the rhythm of daily chapel services. The intellectual rigor of the academy invigorated me. We're told to find our passion; I found mine.

The longer I was at the seminary, the more an aspiration took hold of me: What if I could follow in the footsteps of the most influential people in my life? My teachers shaped me in profound ways. They fostered in me a life of prayer, respect for the church's past, and zeal for the truth. Becoming a professor, holding the clay of future pastors in my own hands, molding them and, by extension, the broader church, seemed to me the ideal vocation.

I noticed instructors dropping subtle hints about a future career I might have at the seminary. My final year, a professor attached a personal note at the end of my term paper for his class. "I look forward," he wrote, "to you teaching alongside me as a fellow faculty member someday." Those words solidified my desires. That would be my future, I decided. And this goal, over time, elbowed its way past others until it climbed onto the throne of my mind, took its seat, and began to rule.

ALL OF US HAVE OUR DAYDREAMS. We envision ourselves standing in the future, where we've accomplished what we set out to do. We worked hard to get there. Maybe it took years of school, followed by long workweeks and countless sacrifices, but we finally arrived. We made something of ourselves. We're people who don't just live, but whose lives are worth something. Others will remember our success, even be jealous of it.

If that's you, then you know what was going through my mind back in those seminary days. You also know what it means when such goals seize control of our lives.

In the summer of 1997, saying good-bye to seminary, my wife and I packed up our belongings and headed west to a new chapter in our lives. A small congregation in a tiny Oklahoma town had called me to serve them. Over the next five years, our lives became intertwined with the lives of the people there. I had been a husband; now I became a pastor. And over time, when my wife and I were blessed with the birth of a daughter, then a son, I became a father as well.

A husband, a pastor, a father. That's who I was. But inwardly I was defined by what I wanted to become: a seminary professor. Everything else I was, every other vocation I held, was strong-armed into the service of achieving this goal.

I wouldn't be able to become a professor unless I had

a strong marriage and a healthy family life, so I tried to be a good husband and a good father. I wouldn't be attractive to the seminary unless I kept the congregation on the theological straight and narrow, so I poured myself into the parish ministry. As I constructed and polished this image of myself, it never dawned on me that those I was called to love and serve had been reduced by me and my daydream to utility: tools to achieve my personal goal.

The opportunity to achieve that goal came quickly. One day, while I sat in my study, the phone rang: the president of the seminary I had attended was on the line. One of the faculty members had unexpectedly resigned midway through the academic year. They needed someone to fill his position. And I was their man.

I flew in for an interview with the board of regents, informed my congregation of the subsequent job offer, and began to make plans to move with my family. In a matter of weeks, I was transported from the pulpit to the front of a seminary classroom where, a few years earlier, I had been a student.

At thirty-one years old, I was the youngest member of the faculty. Soon I settled into my place in this new world. I taught Hebrew and Old Testament classes. I established my identity, found my voice, began to carve out a niche for myself. My new position attracted interest in my writing, and my denomination's publishing house provided ample writing opportunities. Conference planning committees contacted me to serve as speaker or preacher at upcoming events. After a couple of years at the seminary, I was also accepted into the doctoral program at Hebrew Union College. Both a graduate student and a professor: it was the ideal combination. My life was working out just the way I'd wanted it to.

Everything was falling into place.

And as it did, everything also began falling apart.

ONE OF THE IRONIES OF LIFE is that the things we want most are often the very things that destroy us. The longer I taught at the seminary, the more I was asked to write, the more speaking engagements I booked, the more pride ballooned within me. I practiced the art of feigned humility; I downplayed my success. But whatever ruse I used outwardly to conceal my ever-fattening ego actually strengthened my pride, blinding me to the hazards ahead.

Most wives are keen observers of their husbands' nature, aware of the hidden reefs beneath the dark waters their husbands sail. And my wife was no exception. But I was deaf to her admonitions, frustrated by what I perceived as her attempts to stifle my achievements.

What she sensed was the reversal taking place inside me. The teaching position I had once dreamed of, but didn't feel worthy of, now became the job I felt entitled to. I began to see teaching not as a vocation to which God had called me, but as an accomplishment well earned. Gifts were transmogrified into trophies.

It was only when I studied the wreckage of my life years later that I realized all this. At the time, all I knew was that this small-town Texas boy, the first college graduate in his family, had done rather well for himself. I could go home with my head held high. The ladder I had climbed rung by rung had finally brought me to the top. At last I could drop my guard. I had made it.

When everything is going as planned, the sun doesn't seem to set at all. We chart our course, map out our life, and the sun shines on as we live out our dream. I could see the future clearly: I would eventually be Dr. Bird, become a tenured professor, and retire at the seminary. The map had led me here, where I would be safe. And in this safe place, wrapped in the delusion of invincibility, I played with fire.

ALMOST FIVE YEARS TO THE DAY after I moved to the seminary—then a husband, a father of two young children, a pastor, a professor, a speaker, an author—I sat alone on the floor of a one-bedroom apartment. I held a .357 Magnum in my hand and stared into the dark barrel. My wife had moved across the country to live with her parents; soon she would file for divorce. I had watched my weeping son and daughter wave at me through the windows of a car as it drove away. I had tendered my letter of resignation to the seminary, packed up, and moved to another city. My bishop had phoned me to politely ask that I resign from the clergy roster of our church. One by one, various people emailed me to cancel my speaking engagements with them. And the president of the publishing house informed me I would no longer be writing for them.

It wasn't just that my dreams, one by one, had come untrue, but that my life was now haunted by the dreams I trampled underfoot. As I sat alone on that apartment floor, I rocked back and forth and began to weep, then to laugh. A hysterical, demonic laugh shorn of humor, drunk with desperation, from the depths of my self-dug grave.

Sin: predictable in its destructive power while unpredictable in its messiness. You just don't know how many broken pieces there will be, and where all those pieces will land. Years later, after my sins had finally and fully exploded, I was still finding broken shards scattered in the recesses of my life.

I had hosted a party, inviting every vice. Pride was there in full regalia, as were contempt and arrogance. And a lack of love for my neighbor. And selfishness in my marriage, vocation, and friendships. And then a new guest showed up. Lust conceived flirtation, fascination, and desire, which, fully grown, became adultery.

Infidelity always has its genesis in lies. Lies about the innocence of flirtation. Lies about deserving a little more happiness. Lies about "we'll only do this once." Lies that say no one will ever know. Lies that claim we love the other person. And because adultery begins in lies, it also marshals a legion of lies to guard and perpetuate its existence. The more I became involved with the other woman, the deeper my delusion grew. I became skilled at lying to others. I resorted to manipulation to cover my tracks. I thought this was love, that we belonged together. I lied to myself, convinced that only a little compartment within me was unfaithful while the majority remained true. I told myself I'd never felt so alive. All the while I was killing myself, my marriage, another marriage, and my relationships with countless people who cared about me.

Eventually, the lies were unmasked. So much had

been said and so much had been done that to undo it all seemed beyond a herculean task. It was over. When the car carrying my children drove away, I crouched amidst the ruins. In darkness. In the non-light of a set sun, wishing death would overtake me.

WHEN WE LIE TO OURSELVES, a desperate aloneness overwhelms us. The unfaithful spouse knows this. So does the addict. And the more alone we feel, the more we build walls around ourselves. Of course, I was far from alone in what I experienced. Chances are that scattered throughout the apartment complex where I lived were scores of people with stories like my own. I just didn't know it, nor, to be honest, did I really care at the time. I was too fixated on my own wounds to consider the wounds of others. But they were there, a stone's throw away.

All of us shared a common but isolating grief of a life gone terribly wrong. The addict who had smoked and snorted his way out of multiple jobs and multiple relationships had served at the altar of a narcotic god who always demanded more while giving less. The attractive young lady whose résumé was written on her exposed skin had gradually made a career out of her body, devolving from a visual prostitute at strip clubs to a call girl handed over to the highest bidder. The gambler who had made the casino his home repeatedly bankrupted his family until his wife had enough of his "luck" and left him. The man who had learned he loved alcohol above all else became a husband and father whose tongue, wet by the liquor of choice, would issue words so sharp they sliced his family into shreds.

Don't believe those are the only stories. Other stories are close by, too. Professional pretenders have everyone duped into assuming their house is in order. In one such house, as soon as the husband pulls out of the driveway, his wife pours a cup of coffee and logs on to her secret email account, carrying on an emotional affair with an old flame from college. In another house, the dad, known and respected in the community, runs the little community of his household with a sadistic, domineering fist, offering approval only when there's complete submission to his will. His wife hides bruises, and his children hide from fear. In yet another house, when the teenage son finally opens up about his attraction to other boys, his parents shame him into silence and threaten expulsion from the house if he ever mentions the deviancy again. On and on the stories unfold. Inside the innumerable houses that look like Norman Rockwell paintings on the outside, many of us have concealed prisons of absence, abuse, hatred, shaming, anger, resentment, and silent screams.

We all know stories like these. Some of us are living them. You have your story; I have mine. But they all sing, in various tones, a story that started with the sun at full zenith in the sky.

IT'S IMPORTANT TO REALIZE that stories of pain and failure are in us and all around us, because they have been with us from the dawn of humanity. They are the stories written throughout our Scripture. From the opening book of the Bible we come across stories that might be written in our headlines:[1]

"Brother Murders Brother in a Fit of Jealous Rage"

"Spiritual Leader Discovered Drunk
and Naked in His Home"

"Husband's Lies Place Wife
in Danger of Sexual Assault"

"Militants Kidnap Family during Raid"

"Wife Lets Husband Father a Child with the Maid"

"Gang of Men Attempt to Rape a Man's Guests"

"Two Daughters Impregnated by
Inebriated Father"

"Twin Brother Deceives Blind Father
and Steals from Absent Brother"

"Man in Polygamous Household Faces
Constant Family Strife"

"Mass Slaughter Perpetrated by Brothers
to Avenge Sister's Rape"

"Eldest Son Sleeps with His Father's Lover"

"Jealous Brothers Sell Younger Brother
into Slavery"

These are only a sampling from Genesis. As the
scriptural story unfolds, the depths of humanity's selfishness and depravity unfold as well. What's more,
the individuals involved in these tragedies are ordi-
narily not outside the community of believers. They
are church folks. They know who the true God is. They

worship at his altar or tabernacle, and they have received his blessings. Often they are the political or spiritual leaders of the nation. These same people tell lies that derail relationships. They cheat and steal, trick and murder. They get drunk, get angry, get even. And when they do, there is inevitable fallout. They harm themselves, and their families are usually collateral damage.

One of the most shocking aspects of the biblical story is that we find no whitewash on these narratives. No editing out of embarrassing scenes from the recorded lives of God's children. No excuses for why they acted the way they did, nor pointing out of extenuating circumstances. Generation after generation of readers are exposed to the raw, unfiltered truth of the people of God as they were breaking bad.

THAT EVIL IS NOT A NOVELTY in human history might seem hardly worth mentioning. Solomon pointed it out long ago, writing, "There is nothing new under the sun."[2] So what if bloodshed began immediately after the expulsion from Eden? So what if Noah got drunk, Abraham lied, and Judah hired a would-be prostitute? What do these stories reveal that we don't already know?

They reveal a remarkable truth we need to hear over

and over again: God specializes in broken people. He has a long history of being intimately and graciously involved in the lives of people who screw up on a large scale. No matter how badly we have wrecked our lives, our Father is in the thick of that disaster to begin the work of making us whole again.

I didn't always realize this. When I was teaching and preaching, I focused on family-friendly stories of the Lord's people: pious youths standing up to ungodly kings, warriors routing foreign armies, prophets zealous to proclaim God's word. Frankly, I cherry-picked narratives from the Scriptures I wanted to hear. Highlighting the accounts of people whom I sought to emulate, I believed if I were brave enough, strong enough, and faithful enough, I too could push forward to victory.

In focusing on the good stories of good people doing good things, I failed to see the "bad" stories of biblical people whose selfish actions are no occasional footnote. They're the core story of who they—and we—are. We're *homo incurvatus in se*, man turned in on himself.[3] And as in the lives of biblical people, so in our daily lives, we have a God who is turned outward toward us. He searches for the lost sheep and rejoices to carry it home. The Shepherd comes to us in our tears and confusion, as we hold in our hands the shattered remains of the lives we once knew, and begins his most important work in our hearts.

WE'RE AT THE BEGINNING of our journey together, so there is much to say. But the message woven through these chapters is this: Every step of the way we are accompanied by the God who, in Jesus Christ, will never un-love us, un-adopt us, un-redeem us. No matter what we've done, no matter what fallout from our actions has decimated our lives, no matter how much spite or malice, grief or pain, bitterness or despair we feel, we have a God who is on our side. He's walked this path with countless people before us. Now he walks it with us. And there's no better companion than the God who was once called the friend of sinners.

CHAPTER TWO

Reliving Genesis 1 in a FedEx Trailer

WHEN I WAS GROWING UP, there was a story my dad repeated many times. He relayed it as practical knowledge, a bit of wisdom about paying close attention to the lay of the land. He grew up in west Texas, a region better known for what it doesn't have than what it does. It boasts no mountains or rolling hills, no lush vegetation. The trees stand as lonely sentinels in a desolate country, home to cotton farmers and the long-eared, lightning-fast jackrabbit.

Pursuit of that animal was a favorite pastime of my dad and his friends when they were teenagers. Come sundown, they'd load up the pickup with their greyhounds and head to a swath of country nearby. They'd drive for hours on the ruts zigzagging through acres of sand and mesquites. One of the guys would scan the fields with a spotlight to catch the glowing eyes of a jackrabbit. When he spotted one, the dogs would bound out of the pickup, and the race was on. Well after midnight, all tuckered out, the boys would head for home.

One day, my dad and his buddies decided to switch things up and try a daytime hunt. There, in those fields they had driven through a million times in the darkness, they became disoriented in the daylight. The landmarks, the lay of the land, the twists and turns of the ruts—it was as if they'd never seen them before. This place was a radically different world. Nothing looked the same. At every fork in the road, neither left nor right seemed familiar.

They had been at home in the darkness, but they were lost in the light.

It was during this hunt that my father gained this valuable insight, later passing it on to me. As a boy, I knew it as a story; as a man, I came to understand it as a parable of the human condition.

WHEN MY MARRIAGE ENDED in divorce and my career ended in disgrace, I sought shelter in the darkness. For my dad and his friends, the dark hunting fields of west Texas were a place to escape the boredom of everyday life and have a little fun. But for me, the darkness became a sanctuary.

When our lives have been fragmented by self-destructive actions, the light makes us feel lost and afraid, but in the darkness, we begin to feel at home. We're safe. Here we can hide from the shock of what we've done, convince ourselves we still exercise a little control over our lives, and—as strange as it sounds—even begin to decorate the darkness.

In the months following the wreck of my divorce and my resignation from the seminary and the ministry, nothing terrified me more than the truth. Infidelity as a husband, selfishness as a father, betrayal of trust as a pastor and professor and friend—it was all surreal, as if someone else had done these things while inhabiting my skin. I didn't want to own up to any of them. These were the kinds of things other people did.

At dusk I would stand alone on my apartment balcony. Let the deepening darkness envelop me. Shiver in the cold. Repeat to myself that none of this was happening. And as long as I was in the darkness, the words seemed believable.

WE ARE MAKERS of our own little worlds. This is the illusion we can trace back to the beginning of humanity's story. The serpent said to Adam and Eve, "You will be like God, knowing good and evil," assuring them of a divine degree of control over their lives.[1] The Lord created the heavens and the earth, and we, in the God-like state, usurped them for ourselves. And over these self-made worlds we seek to wield absolute control.

It's easier to live by this creed when the plan we have for our lives is falling into place instead of falling apart. That for so many years I had seemed able to fashion my own little world only deepened my belief in this lie. If I earned the right degrees, behaved the right way, and shook the right hands, then what I desired would come to pass. With my lips I said, "God is directing my life," but in my heart I said, "This is my self-made world."

When our lives collapse, we tighten our grip on the lie. When Adam and Eve's perfect world was collapsing around them, when their eyes were opened, they saw their nakedness. Their very first action was to try to take control of the situation by covering themselves: "They sewed fig leaves together and made themselves loincloths."[2]

What this first couple did not do is just as significant as what they did. They did not acknowledge the truth of what they had done. They recognized that their lives were fundamentally altered, but they refused to turn to the very one who, in love, had fashioned them. After succumbing to sin, they immediately tried to hide its effects. Their eyes were opened, but their hearts were closed. And in these dark, secret chambers, they decided what their next move would be. They would manage the mess. They would do damage control.

This control first took the form of making coverings for themselves. Hilarity and sadness intermingle in this action. They supposed that leaves from a fig tree were a sufficient cover-up. In their panic and shame, they grasped at something, anything, to undo what was, in fact, undoable. By acting in this way, they underscored the desperate nature of their predicament. Supposing they were taking control, they painted in bold relief how out of control they really were.

"[W]E LOVE THE SAFETY of the darkness over the violence of the light," writes A. J. Swoboda. "Light is scary. It exposes the monsters."[3] We fear these truth-monsters, so we refuse to relinquish control, to demolish our self-made worlds, to lose the identities we have so carefully crafted for ourselves. In our newfound sanctuary, we hide from what we've done. We grapple for words to describe our fear and grief and rage. A language of the languishing. But in the dark, we find none. All we have is the language of the lie.

Still, determined to stay, we begin to decorate this

darkness in which we reside. These decorations vary from person to person, but they all indicate our desire to remain where we are. "Home is where the heart is," so we will transform this darkness into our new abode.

Sometimes these decorations remind us of the people we once were. They're mementoes of previous accomplishments we used to define our worth. One of mine was a small piece of hardened plastic imprinted with these words: "Prof. Chad L. Bird." Formerly the nameplate attached to my office door at the seminary, now the sign was taped to the wall above my desk, in my line of vision. The sign did more than anchor me to that period of my life. It told me I once had been somebody, accomplished something.

Remembrance wasn't the problem; it was the ongoing pride it engendered. In my darkened state, this nameplate stamped my current life with a past importance. Through it I relived my "glory days," as the Bruce Springsteen song goes. I gazed with admiration at myself, at the man I had once been.

Sometimes decorations take the form of rituals of regret. Not the regret akin to repentance, but egocentric regret enacted in our sanctuaries of darkness. Whatever the rituals, their focus is not on how we've injured others, but on licking our own wounds. Or, to put it more precisely, on biting our own wounds. For it is not healing we seek but the perpetuation of pain.

Over time, a sadistic state of mind began to overpower me in the darkness. I didn't want healing. I wanted gaping, bleeding wounds. I desired hurt, for in it I sought to atone for what I'd done. This hurt is another form of seeking control. In performing rituals of regret, we search for an atonement in which we're the sacrificial victim.

After my family left, I took a part-time job loading FedEx trucks on the evening shift. For four to six hours every night, in a sweaty, monotonous rhythm, I would stand in a trailer and stack box upon box, make wall after wall of cardboard. In my mind, I stacked thought upon thought. I built a wall of atonement. I will be forgiven, I thought, when I am sufficiently sorry for what I have done. I will bleed out on the altar of shame. I will relive in my mind, again and again, the mistakes I have made. If I hate myself enough for my actions, maybe God will love me.

Rituals of regret are pervaded by the "I." I will do this, I will do that, and I will be okay again. In these liturgies, both the worshiper and the worshiped are the same: the ego. "We strive all our life to see ourselves as keepers of rules we cannot keep, as loyal subjects

of laws under which we can only be judged outlaws,"
writes Robert Farrar Capon. "Yet so deep is our need
to derive our identity from our own self-respect—so
profound is our conviction that unless we watch our
step, the watchbird will take away our name—that we
will spend a lifetime trying to do the impossible rather
than, for even one carefree minute, consent to having
it done for us by someone else."[4]

THE LONGER WE RESIDE in this darkness, the more we
are also tempted to decorate our lives with additional
layers of darkness, given the army of desires warring
within. Defeated in this war over and over again, I began
to self-medicate by reaching for a bottle of Jim Beam. I
sought the forgetfulness the rapidly emptying bottles on
my kitchen counter brought. And I sought distraction
from my grief in the arms of the opposite sex, in the temporary euphoria afforded by the delusion of "falling in
love." In different women's arms, and in their beds, I not
only felt physical pleasure that offset my spiritual pain,
but I felt better about myself. I craved their affirmation,
their acceptance. "She says she loves me, wants me," I
told myself, "so I must be a better person than I feel like
I am." Just as I used drinking to forget, I used girlfriends
to intoxicate myself with sex and emotional entangle-

ments. So long as my mind was focused on distraction, it was less prone to reflect upon who I had become.

All of these decorations of darkness served to anchor me to an existence I was afraid to give up. Because I was enslaved to darkness, I couldn't imagine a life of light. I became like the Israelites, who didn't want to leave their slavery in Egypt. When Moses told them the Lord wanted to free them, be their God, and bring them back to the land of promise, they refused to listen to him "because of their broken spirit and harsh slavery."[5] They told him, "Leave us alone that we may serve the Egyptians."[6] Even after they were freed, they lamented ever leaving Egypt, making plans to return to servitude there.[7] I understand that feeling. Broken in spirit, fearing liberation, I was content to stay a prisoner in the little Egypt of my shattered life.

Liberation is frightening to anyone who has become so accustomed to captivity.

Yes, the darkness is attractive because in it we can hide from the full shock of what we've done. Yes, in darkness we can maintain the illusion of control. And, yes, we can decorate our jail cells so they feel more like home. But the underlying reason for the powerful draw of darkness is distinct from all of these.

Those of us suffering from addiction, criminal behavior, promiscuity, a divorce, or any other manifold catastrophe ruining our lives—we gravitate toward the darkness for one primary reason: we are afraid to die. I don't mean the kind of death where our hearts stop beating and our lungs quit breathing. I'm talking about a deeper, deadlier death: the death of the people we have created ourselves to be, the people we assume we must be in order for God to accept and love us.

I HAD LIVED MY LIFE in a constant state of self-creation. In my interactions with others, in my chosen enterprises, in my conquests and defeats, I had always been shaping myself. I had an image in mind I strove to achieve. Right now you're reading the story of my self-creation. And you have your own story as well. But all our stories have one thing in common: all of us grapple with seeking divine approval through human effort, whether we realize it or not.

We engage in this self-creation for various reasons, and not all are bad. But bleeding through every one of them is an assumed falsehood: We suppose there must be something about us—good or even not so good—that makes God stop and take notice of us. Maybe we can make ourselves smart, rich, beautiful, popular, or athletic. Maybe we can be pious, religious, charitable, zealous, prayerful, or conservative. Or maybe we're down-and-out, lonely, wounded, weak, or grieving.

One person says to himself, "God will notice me because I'm a widower." Another, "God will notice me because I've worked for the church." Still another, "God will notice me because I speak up for moral causes." They all sound different, but they're all the same. We're seeking identity, acceptance, and the divine nod of approval because of what we've created or embraced.

Even hiding in darkness, we're engaged in the work of self-creation. I know, because I told myself I'd re-create a smaller version of who I was before: Relocate, teach at a community college, carve out a niche for myself. I could be the old me in a new place. Maybe we even try to act out, make ourselves so bad that we're sure God will *have* to take notice of us. I did this, too. Every empty bottle, every stranger's bed of crumpled sheets was a cry for heaven to look down and see how far I'd fallen. However we create and sustain these identities, they are precious to us because we mistake them for life. And because of this, our greatest fear is the death of those people we have created ourselves to be.

THIS IS THE WAY IT IS in the world. Who gets noticed, accepted, celebrated? The people who stand out. We know the names of the powerful. We feel compassion for the victims whose stories are familiar. We see something in them that sparks love or mercy or acceptance. But we have no pageants for alley-dwellers, no fundraisers for the anonymous. We learn this pattern, internalize it. And we reason that as we are, so God is.

Only God isn't. God sees us most clearly when we feel most invisible. The Psalmist asks, "Who is like the LORD our God, who is seated on high, who looks far down on the heavens and the earth?"[8] As God gazes down from on high, his focus rests on a different group, the poor and the needy: "He raises the poor from the dust, and lifts the needy from the ash heap, to make them sit with princes, with the princes of his people."[9] Those whom the world overlooks, God looks over with tender care. Those who lift themselves heavenward, as it were, are far from God, while those who sink low are near to him.

Mary says it best in the *Magnificat*, where she sings that God "has looked on the humble estate of his servant. . . . He has scattered the proud in the thoughts of their hearts; he has brought down the mighty from their thrones and exalted those of humble estate."[10] Commenting on this, Martin Luther says, "For since He is the Most High, and there is nothing above Him, He cannot look above Him; nor yet to either side, for there is none like Him. He must needs, therefore, look within Him and beneath Him; and the farther one is beneath Him, the better does He see him."[11] He is a far-sighted God. "In fact," Luther goes on, "sometimes He even lets us fall into sin, in order that He may look into the depths even more, bring help to many, perform manifold works, show Himself a true Creator, and thereby make Himself known and worthy of love and praise."[12]

I myself was completely blind to how God was at work in my life to deflate my pride. He was pushing me downward, to a lower place, so he could see me more clearly. His first step was pushing me out of a seminary lecture hall and into a FedEx trailer.

In this lower place, I died. I experienced the death we all fear most—the death of the people we have created ourselves to be. The successful, prideful professor at the front of the classroom was dead. I was uncreated. I became an anonymous loader of cardboard boxes. I was nothing. But I was the material God uses for creation—and re-creation. God is not a craftsman who utilizes other products to make something new. He creates ex nihilo, out of nothing. So he makes into nothing those of us who thought ourselves to be something.

This reversal is God's way of reshaping us into the

people he wants us to be, as Luther goes on to say in his commentary on the Magnificat:

> Just as God at the beginning of creation made the world out of nothing, whence He is called the Creator and the Almighty, so His manner of working continues unchanged. Even now and to the end of the world, all His works are such that out of that which is nothing, worthless, despised, wretched, and dead, He makes that which is something, precious, honorable, blessed, and living. On the other hand, whatever is something, precious, honorable, blessed, and living, He makes to be nothing, worthless, despised, wretched, and dying.[13]

This is the death we fear most, and need most.

This is the death we fear because it strips us of everything we are proud of, defined by. I had no wall of fame in those trailers I was loading. No audience, no applause. Just sweat, dirt, and boxes.

God was teaching me that I was utterly out of control. He was leading me to realize I couldn't excuse myself for what I did. I was dying to my self-creation. This is the death that makes us nothing. But with all our labor of self-creation undone, God can move forward with his work of creation out of the nothing we have become.

WE DON'T SEE IT AT THE TIME, but this is the love of God at work in us. As Gerhard Forde says, "It is love, the love of God that creates out of nothing, calls into being that which is from that which is not. This love of God that creates its object is contrasted absolutely with the love of humans."[14] Forde is echoing what Luther says about the uniqueness of God's love for us: "The love of God that lives in man loves sinners, evil persons, fools, and weaklings in order to make them righteous, good, wise, and strong. Rather than seeking its own good, the love of God flows forth and bestows good. Therefore sinners are attractive because they are loved; they are not loved because they are attractive."[15]

It is out of love that God, who brought creation into being out of nothing, recreates us from the nothing we have become so that we are the people he desires us to be. God began my own Genesis 1 in the back of a 53-foot trailer, in an industrial section of Cincinnati, Ohio. I felt like I was in hell. My Father knew it was just a different sort of Eden.

As I discovered after a long time, the death of self we fear most gives way to the life we need most. It's in the darkness that God reveals his light. "Even the darkness is not dark to you," the Psalmist says; "the night is as bright as the day."[16] We may conceal ourselves in the dark, we may decorate the darkness, but midnight is noon to our Father. He will seek us out, as a shepherd searches for his lost sheep. And there's no boundary he won't cross to find us.

For those of us who are now crouching down in the darkness, or who still sometimes feel its allure, living in the darkness will seem easier than living in the light. But it's an ease that slowly chokes life away. I know it well. For years, darkness was my foul jail cell. I wore my fig leaf, bit my wounds, cradled my precious mementoes of a lost past. I intoxicated myself with sin. And I feared the freedom and love and forgiveness of life in the light.

But the Son of God continues to leap into the darkness with a wild and reckless love. He storms our cells that reek of decomposition. He pries open our fingers to take away the lies to which we cling. Then he picks us up and carries us out into the light. At first, it hurts. It's blinding. It's too free. But he holds us there. To our trembling hearts, he whispers, "Listen, I have never stopped loving you. Your past no longer defines you.

You are forgiven. My peace, my hope, my Father, my everything is yours."

These are the words of our liberation. In Christ, our crucified Brother, we are freed to be the children of our heavenly Father. Now, decorated by the light, with the righteousness of Christ, we are blessedly lost in a love that knows no limitations.

Adam and Eve's act of hiding revealed their sin.

CHAPTER THREE

Where the Hell Are You, God?

S OME LOSSES IN LIFE are so abrupt and cataclysmic that our initial response is to deny their existence. A policeman at the door with news of a car crash that's claimed the life of our loved one. The doctor coming back into the room to tell us the tumor is malignant. If we can speak at all, our mouths erupt with a long litany of No's. The pain is too monumental for us to bear, so we take refuge in denial. For how long? A day, a month, a year? For as long as we can. Until all the No's trail off into silence. Until finally there's nothing left for us to do but face the cold, hard truth.

All my denials finally reached their expiration date in the summer of 2007. My wife and I had separated; she and our children had moved back to Texas to live with her parents. Over the next twelve months, my life was punctuated with a series of funerals: the seminary job, the teaching career, the ministry, countless friendships, and finally my marriage—all entombed. Every few weeks, my shovel dug a fresh grave. And with each burial, my ability to exist in ongoing denial weakened. At first it all seemed like a dream—a nightmarish dream, but still a dream—but I was gradually waking up.

Finally, one day, I did.

This awakening happened worlds away from the life I had known. It was in the cab of a Mack truck, in the oil fields of the Texas Panhandle, in the dead of night.

The time and distance away from my children had been too painful, both for me and for them. So after my string of foolish decisions, I finally made a wise one. I walked away from plans to land another teaching position and began a radically different kind of career, one that would enable me to live near my children and remain an active part of their lives.

I became a truck driver.

THE BREAD AND BUTTER of the little Texas town where my children were living was oil and gas. The jobs were there. So I underwent training to earn my commercial driver's license, loaded a U-Haul to the gills, moved into an apartment in that town, and was hired by a local company to pull a tanker. I was on the clock about seventy hours a week. Being the new guy, I was stuck on the graveyard shift. I bounced along rut-scarred, back-country roads in the darkness, accompanied only by my thoughts. It was the ideal place for reality to catch up with me.

One night it did. After a few weeks on the job, all my denials withered to nothing. My hands, so accustomed to resting on a pulpit or a lectern, grasped the steering wheel of a truck. They were stained with oil and grease. My ring finger was un-ringed. I wore a blue-collar work shirt; my clericals would never see the light of day again. On my head was a hardhat, and on my feet, steel-toed boots. I had no wife waiting at home for me. My children wouldn't run up to greet me when I got off work. My daily planner, once so essential, was in the trash. There were no books to review, no articles to write, no conferences to attend, no classes to teach, no phone calls to return. I was grateful to live close to my children, but I still felt like a disgraced, defeated man.

Worse, I felt like God had abandoned me. Or I had abandoned him. Or we had both grown sick of each other's company. I didn't know which of these came closer to the truth. All I knew was that I had become a persona non grata in God's club. His angelic bouncers had thrown me into the street. If I were the man on the road to Jericho in Jesus's parable, lying there half-dead, God either walked on by me while whistling Dixie, or came over to give me a swift kick in the groin before going on his merry way. This much was clear: heaven didn't give a damn about me. I had sinned too much, angered the Almighty too long, hurt too many people, burned too many bridges. This became my creed.

I cannot fully sympathize with many things in life because I haven't experienced them myself. But this godforsaken feeling—this I know well. I know how it tastes, smells, and looks. For years, my heart's address was that hellhole.

LET ME START where denial ends. When we've finally begun to face reality, when all our initial No's grow mute, what is left to say? Not pious-sounding prayers. What we need is a language free of all fluffy, feel-good religious blather. But how can we translate our emotions of anger, desperation, and disappointment into nouns and verbs? We can't even voice where we are, where we feel God is, until we have speech giving utterance to the unutterable. We need to be taught a language that's hard, jagged, honest, and raw.

I learned that language in the school of the Psalms.

A school that often felt more like a barroom where God and I could brawl. Philip Yancey says, "Doubt, paranoia, giddiness, meanness, delight, hatred, joy, praise, vengefulness, betrayal—you can find it all in the Psalms."[1] I found all that and more. I discovered raw words, real words. With these I both grieved God's absence and protested his attacks. All the emotions swirling around within me escaped as harsh words thrown at heaven. I gave vent to my sense of abandonment, cried out from my despair.

On the long drives at night, I found in the Psalms what I had been searching for: the language of the languishing. The Psalms place words on our lips so critical of God they border on blasphemy. They translate our suffering into speech, yes, but they also translate God's seeming absence into a surprising presence. The Psalms reveal a God who, though he feels worlds away from us, is as close as the marrow in our bones. In every syllable of the Psalms, the magnitude of the Father's compassion is mysteriously present to guide us when we feel blind and to love us when we seem unlovable.

Still, some of the images in the Psalms look like a backdrop for a horror movie. Psalm 88 is especially graphic. The poet grieves that he's trapped in a hellish tomb where his only comrades are corpses. He is "in the regions dark and deep." His beloved and his friends shun him; his only companion is darkness. But this isn't bad luck; it's not as if fate has dealt him a sorry hand. The Psalmist points an accusing finger upward and rails at God: "You have put me in the depths of the pit." "You overwhelm me with all your waves." "You have caused my companions to shun me." "You surround me like a flood all day long." In this prayer, God is wearing the colors of the enemy.[2] In the copy of the Psalms I carried in my truck, this rant had my dirty fingerprints all over it.

 This brash, candid prayer doesn't stand alone. It's one example among many in the Psalms. Taking a panoramic shot of the entire collection, we see a range of dark images: God has shepherded his flock to the slaughterhouse, sold his people for chump change, made Israel the butt of their enemies' jokes.[3] The Lord has made his people drunk with destruction; they stagger about in the stupor of suffering.[4] Divine anger smokes against the sheep of his pasture.[5] He has fed his people "with the bread of tears and given them tears to drink in full measure."[6] He has "cast off and rejected" them, renounced his covenant with them, and thrown the regal crown into the dirt.[7]

But we meet more than anger and lament. The

Psalmist also floods the heavens with probing questions: Where is God? Why is all this happening to us? How long will God drag his feet before he acts? For instance, "Why, O LORD, do you stand afar off? Why do you hide yourself in times of trouble?"[8] Or, "How long, O LORD? Will you reject me forever? How long will you hide your face from me? How long must I take counsel in my soul and have sorrow in my heart all the day?"[9] Or, "O God, why do you cast us off forever?"[10] This series of rapid-fire questions from Psalm 77 sums it up best:

> Will the LORD spurn forever, and never be favorable
>   again?
> Has his steadfast love forever ceased?
> Are his promises at an end for all time?
> Has God forgotten to be gracious?
> Has he in anger shut up his compassion?[11]

The poet sees nothing but a sky-high iron wall between himself and God.

I BEGAN READING the Psalms when I parked my rig at gas wells during the lonely hours of the night. I turned off the headlights, killed the engine, and flipped on the cab lights. They shone down on the pages of the Bible as it rested on the steering wheel. Here in the oil field, I met what I never met in Sunday school. Here were harsh and bitter prayers, honest and real. They bled truth. They translated the angst and anger I felt toward the God who'd made a sport of me, spit in my face, and kicked me to the curb.

Their brutal honesty came as a welcome shock. So often we don't know what to say. Or we're fearful of saying too much or the wrong thing. The Psalms not only allow us to let go but tell us not to keep our frustration bottled up. They encourage us to pop the cork, to give full vent to our woe. God isn't waiting with a baseball bat to brain us when we pray these words. He's given them to us so that we can shout and cry them back to him. So I did. Inside my truck cab, I hurled the Psalms at heaven.

There's a time for Hallelujahs, and there's a time for "Where the hell are you, God?" That was the brooding question hanging over me. I asked it through gritted teeth as I drove my truck during those small hours of the night. I asked it as I sat alone in my house and stared blankly at the walls. One afternoon, I screamed it as I drove by a local church where the parking lot was packed with vehicles. It was the day my ex-wife was marrying another man. Then I asked it as I watched my children growing up with him as their stepfather, and with me as just an every-other-weekend presence in their lives.

And you? When do you ask, "Where the hell are you, God? How long, God? Why, God?"

As I WRESTLED with these questions, people offered me all sorts of advice and answers. They meant well, but their words only led me to spiritual and emotional dead-ends.

One would say, "Sounds like God has enrolled you in the school of hard knocks. He's teaching you how to be more self-reliant." But the very reason for my downfall was self-reliance. If God was teaching me anything, it certainly wasn't to lean on myself.

Another told me to take comfort in the omnipresence of God, to know that since he is everywhere, he was certainly with me in my suffering. That has the ring of truth, but it's ultimately as meaningless as saying to the man dying of thirst, "Water is everywhere on the globe, so just go find the nearest faucet and drink up."

Most people would tell me something along these lines: "Listen—eventually, it'll all be okay. God is in control of your life. He has a plan for you. You just don't see it now." Again, this advice sounded true—but it was packed with seeds ultimately blossoming into despair.

What if I never see why all this happened? What then? Is this what it feels like when God is in control? Then I'd hate to see what happens if he ever loses control.

The problem is, we're hardwired to demand answers to questions which, if provided, would do nothing more than perplex us and plunge us further into disappointment. We would be like eight-year-olds trying to understand Einstein lecturing on the theory of relativity. Here's the simple truth: The undisclosed ways of God remain locked in a vault to which we don't have the combination. "The secret things belong to the LORD our God, but the things that are revealed belong to us and to our children."[12] As much as we want to pry into these secret things, they're not really what we need.

How God is controlling the details of our lives is beyond our concern as well as our comprehension. We don't need to hear "God is in control of your life" or "He has a wonderful plan for you."

We need to hear the unheard voice always praying in concert with us. As we moan in our sorrow, object to our abandonment, and question where God is, we never do so alone. The words we use have always been the words of another. I'm not talking about David, Solomon, the sons of Korah, or any other poet in the Psalms.

But the one on whose lips every psalm is fully true: our brother and fellow sufferer, Jesus.

AT THE FULCRUM of his excruciating pain, Jesus cried out, "My God, my God, why have you forsaken me?"[13] Jesus didn't pray this to click off one more fulfilled prophecy of his saving work. This was a true, gut-wrenching prayer. It erupted not merely from a tortured body, but from a heart that felt forsaken by the Father. And compressed within this singular question are the other probing interrogatives of the Psalms. Jesus could well have cried out, "Why do you hide yourself in times of trouble?"[14] "How long, O LORD? Will you reject me forever? How long will you hide your face from me?"[15] "Has God forgotten to be gracious?"[16] And, indeed, he did pray them, for "My God, my God, why . . ." embodies them all.

When we pray these same words, our lips move with Christ's, our tears flow into the same stream. We are one with him, and he with us.

"The Psalter is the prayer book of Jesus Christ in the truest sense of the word," Dietrich Bonhoeffer reminds us.[17] "The One who is here protesting his innocence, who is invoking God's judgment, who has come to such infinite depths of suffering, is none other than Jesus Christ himself. He it is who is praying here, and not only here but in the whole Psalter."[18] He is the one who asks, "Where the hell are you, God? How long, God? Why, God?" He is the one whose "life draws near to Sheol,"[19] whose food is "the bread of tears."[20] He is the anointed one who is "cast off and rejected," against whom God is "full of wrath."[21]

And, astonishingly, Jesus is even the one who prays the psalms of confession and repentance. He confesses our guilt as his own because God has made him to be sin on our behalf.[22] As our Savior he prays, "Sacrifice and offering you have not desired, but you have given me an open ear," and as our substitute he prays a few verses later, "My iniquities have overtaken me."[23] At the Last Supper he prays, "Even my close friend in whom I trusted, who ate my bread, has lifted up his heel against me," and in the same psalm he prays as our substitute, "O LORD, be gracious to me; heal me, for I have sinned against you."[24] When we pray Psalm 51, the adulterer and murderer with whom we pray is not only David but Jesus—the righteous one who became our unrighteousness. To say it more accurately, we and David pray in the voice of Jesus, for this psalm, like all other psalms, belongs to him.

ONE NIGHT IN JANUARY, all this began to sink in. When a melting snow had turned every dirt road to mud, I got stuck trying to pull a tank full of waste water up a steep hill. I was a good fifteen miles into the backcountry. No man's land. A guy with a bulldozer was on his way to pull my truck out of the muck, but it would be at least three hours before he could navigate the roads to get near me. So I just sat there. The diesel engine idling. My thoughts racing backward and forward over my life. I reached for my copy of the Psalms and began to read, one after another. I echoed their frustration, their fear, their anger. The raw cries of the ancient words spilled out. And for the first time, late that night, I began to hear the unheard voice of Jesus praying with me and within me.

The Son of God came down to this world of mud and muck and oil-field nights where broken people plead for help. He's there in truck cabs and lonely bedrooms and rehab centers. A song from the nineties asked, "What if God was one of us? Just a slob like one of us?" A God unafraid of slumming with the gang of failures we are. A God who's sunk himself into our humanity while remaining fully divine. A bodied God. The kind of God we need. The kind of God we have in Jesus.

What I've learned to appreciate most about our God of skin and bone is how underwhelming he is. Jesus didn't walk the streets of Nazareth with his face aglow. He looked like the guy at Walmart you push your cart past on the way to get milk. He was no head-turner. "He had no form or majesty that we should look at him," Isaiah says, "no beauty that we should desire him."[25] Maybe Jesus was ugly, or fat, or had bad teeth. He wasn't GQ material. He was the kind of God you could miss, because he hid in plain sight, as a regular Joe—finally even as a convicted criminal sentenced to die.

He was a Psalms kind of man, just as we are a Psalms kind of people. He had enemies out there eager to jump him. He had lonely nights when it seemed he had no friend left in the world. And because he chose to make our sins his own, he was strung up between two thieves, with guilt and regret and shame burning like a bonfire in his bones. He is the God of the Psalms, and the man of the Psalms, in whose life and voice we find a Lord unlike anything we could have planned for.

All of our questions—"Where the hell are you, God?" "How long, God?" "Why, God?"—are finally answered in God's unique way: in the full disclosure of himself in Jesus Christ.

WHEN WE CRY OUT, "How long, O LORD? Will you reject me forever?,"[26] we find the answer not in a timetable where God unveils his plan for our lives, but in the three hours Jesus hung upon the cross. In the man Jesus, we encounter the God who is not our foe but our dearest friend, one who is "able to sympathize with our weaknesses."[27] Author Jessica Thompson describes Christ's sympathy this way: "If you put two pianos in the same room and you strike a note, putting hammer to string, on one of the pianos, the same string on the other piano will vibrate. That is a picture of Christ's heart and our own. If one of his family is hurting, his heart hurts in the same way."[28] His heart and our heart become one.

"But it doesn't feel that way," we might say. No, it doesn't. I get that. Our feelings are unpredictable and unmanageable. They rise and fall. They morph into their kaleidoscope of moods. But no matter how erratic our emotions, our Father is not angry with us in the morning, apathetic at noon, and happy in the evening. Our emotions are constantly in flux, but as Elyse Fitzpatrick writes, God's "love doesn't fluctuate from day-to-day. It was settled the moment he set it upon you before the foundation of the world."[29] His love is the one stable, unchanging reality of our lives.

"Why do you hide yourself in times of trouble?" the Psalmist asks. Just as the glory of God was concealed beneath Jesus, a common-looking man; just as his victory over sin was hidden beneath the shame and blood and suffering of the cross; so God is also veiled beneath the darkness and grief as we travel the crooked path leading from brokenness to healing.

As I discovered, God even hides in Mack trucks.

IT HAS BEEN MANY YEARS since that memorable night when I sat in my semi in the oil field, stared into the darkness, and felt the fearsome reality of my situation take me in its grip. I didn't realize it then, nor would I have believed it if you'd told me, but at the moment when I felt farther from God than I had ever been, he was as close as the breath in my lungs and the blood in my heart.

Unafraid of the darkness, Jesus enters it with us. No matter where we are on this crooked path, we do not walk it alone. In the valley of the shadow of death, Jesus is with us.

CHAPTER FOUR

Burying the Hatchet in an Oil-Field Grave

W HEN PEOPLE ASKED ME what I did for a living, I never told them the whole truth. I'd tell them I drove a truck for a small oil-field company operating a few miles outside of Miami, Texas. I'd tell them I hauled waste water away from gas wells to nearby disposals. And I'd tell them I worked long hours on the night shift, from dusk to dawn. All of that was true, but it wasn't the complete story.

I had a secret vocation. Yes, I would steer the truck and shift gears, hook up hoses and climb tanks. But the job I performed with my hands and feet was one thing; the job I was performing with my mind was quite another. Outwardly, I was engaged in the tasks of a truck driver. Inwardly, I was a spiritual engineer. And I was constructing in my mind a theological edifice of immense proportions, the whole of which was built on sand.

One of the banes and blessings of truck drivers' lives is the inordinate amount of time we have to be alone with our thoughts. Since I worked twelve to fourteen hours a day, I had ample time to think without interruption. And think I did. I thought of all the family, friends, students, and colleagues whom I had hurt and disappointed by my self-serving actions. I thought of God with a mixture of fear, anger, and longing for reacceptance. And I thought of the people who had betrayed me, who had taken advantage of my downfall to heap even more shame and contempt upon me. My mind was a jumble of guilt and disgust, grief and anger, doubt and faith.

In the middle of all these scattered thoughts, however, a center developed around which everything else swirled. That center was forgiveness. How could a holy God possibly forgive me? Should I—and why should I— forgive others? And how could I ever forgive myself?

I came up with my own answers to these questions. But every answer I concocted turned out to be dead wrong. I, the spiritual engineer, built a theology of forgiveness on a foundation of myths.

We easily mistake these myths for truth. After all, they sound like sentiments commonly thrown about in religious circles. They're the kind of language deeply ingrained in our psychological culture. And—most importantly—these myths still allow us to wield some control over the process of forgiveness. Because we have skin in the game, this makes them attractive. And very dangerous.

At one time or another, whether we realize it or not, we've built a theological edifice of our own. We've laid the foundation using these same forgiveness myths, so it's essential we take a close look at them. God exposed them in my own mind, and then used his wrecking ball to demolish them. In their place he built a home of true reconciliation and forgiveness in Christ.

CLIMB INSIDE THE HEAD of one of the most memorable characters in the parables of Jesus: the so-called Prodigal Son. "So-called" because he could be more aptly described as the Conditional Son.

This man amasses an impressive collection of skeletons in his closet. When he demands his inheritance from his father, he's saying, in essence, "Dad, I wish you were dead. But since you're not, let's make-believe you are so I can pocket my inheritance, move out of the house, and go live it up in the world." Astonishingly, the father heeds his request. The son packs a suitcase and soon gets down to the business of squandering "his property in reckless living."[1] You're familiar with the story. He has an impressive rap sheet: he's insulted his father; shamed his family and no doubt made them a laughingstock in the community; wasted his wealth on selfish pleasures; become stoned on the drug of narcissism. He's made himself the center and god of his own pathetic little universe.

When his pockets are empty and a famine plagues the country, he settles for the only job he can find—a feeder of pigs. So raw is his hunger that he longs to drop to his knees and belly up to the trough with the swine. With the bottom fallen out of his world, he too begins to build a theological edifice in his mind.

He makes a decision: he'll go crawling back home. But he can't simply show up on the doorstep, ask that bygones be bygones. He understands that sins have consequences. His father may have been foolish enough to hand over the inheritance, but, as the saying goes, "Fool me once, shame on you. Fool me twice, shame on me." There's no way his dad is simply going to welcome him back home with open arms, no questions asked. But if he does three key things—demonstrates adequate, sincere repentance, humbly accepts a servant position in the household, and gradually earns his father's favor again through a demonstrable life of obedience—then perhaps everything will be made right again.

If he meets all these conditions, he will be fully restored as a son. Should he fail to fulfill any of these conditions, he can kiss the absolution good-bye. While he may be a Prodigal Son, we see he is more accurately a Conditional Son. He has believed the lie that the father's forgiveness—God's forgiveness—is contingent upon pre- and post-conditions. If he leaves these conditions unfulfilled, or not sincerely fulfilled, he will remain unforgiven.

His theology and mine were cut from the same cloth. He constructed this "if-then" theology of forgiveness while feeding pigs. I did it while driving a truck. But we both arrived at the same conclusion.

In the aftermath of career failures, the wreckage of relationships, and recoveries from addiction, many of us embrace this way of thinking. Our Father may welcome us back, but we'll need to earn our place again in the family home. And we'll also need to keep to the straight and narrow afterward. Otherwise, God will snatch away the forgiveness which our repentance, humility, and obedience made possible.

If that's what you think, you're not alone. Nor— thank God!—are you right.

DURING THOSE LONG NIGHTS in the cab of my truck, I was plagued by more than the guilt of my own transgressions. A rage was also building inside me as I recollected the wrongs I had suffered at the hands (and especially the loose lips) of others. It was as if two documentaries were streaming through my mind simultaneously: one recounted, scene by scene, my biography of failures; the other replayed, person after person, those who had hurt me. (Hollywood's most highly acclaimed director couldn't have made more accurate movies than the two I filmed in the studio of my mind)

Many nights on the long roads, I found myself gravitating toward the version documenting the words and actions of those who had kicked me when I was down. Sometimes I would watch that whole movie, then go back to the beginning and watch it again. At other times, I would fast-forward to the climactic scenes and view them in slow motion. I'd hit pause and sit there, drinking in the bitterness, tasting the pain, clenching my fists. I concocted elaborate schemes of revenge. I wrote tirades in my mind that I could scream at my offenders. I dreamed up episodes where I could publicly shame them.

Many of us in that dark valley have had a pair of movies playing through our minds. I had my cast of characters; you had yours. The narratives of each film vary from person to person because each of us has been hurt in different ways. But every movie, no matter how different in details, embodies the same basic questions: (What do I do with this anger and disappointment? Do I seek revenge or grant forgiveness? Or do I attempt an impossible, toxic mixture of the two? Why should I even attempt to forgive? And, if I do, how can I pull it off? What will happen if I do forgive?)

Even when the shouts of anger bellowed within me, I could hear the Spirit of God whispering these questions. I couldn't escape them. None of us can.

Quite effortlessly, we assemble a passel of reasons why we shouldn't forgive others. Maybe the offenders aren't sorry for what they did—or, if they are sorry, they don't show (what we deem to be) adequate remorse. Or we're afraid if we forgive them, they might interpret absolution as a free pass to repeat their behavior. Or we withhold forgiveness punitively, as a weapon of silence to make people pay for what they've done. Or we might simply hate their guts, and decide those lowlifes don't deserve to hear one kind word from us. Whatever our chosen reasons might be, we keep those three words, "I forgive you," buried deep within us.

Lurking behind every reason we don't forgive is one

fundamental impulse: we desire to control the offenders. We might dangle forgiveness in front of them, like
a carrot before a horse, until finally they do our will. Or
we offer to overlook everything if, and only if, they
apologize. Or we decide that the people who've hurt us
need to see our pain, so they themselves feel remorse.
If we forgive them, we'll send the message that we're
okay. But we're not okay, and as long as we're not, they
shouldn't be, either.

In every instance, forgiveness morphs into a self-
serving tool of manipulation we use to control other
people. Inside our clouded minds, we convince ourselves we're doing what's ultimately best for us.

It's NATURAL to self-protect when we've been hurt. But
we take it too far when we vow, "This will never happen
again." That's when we initiate the wall-building cam-
paign, erecting protective barriers around ourselves.
Each one says loud and clear, "Never again." Never
again will I trust a man to be faithful to me. Never again
will I bare my soul to another person. Never again will
I set foot in a church. And to fortify these "never again"
vows, we promise ourselves we'll forgive others only
when such forgiveness will benefit us. It becomes a
weapon in our arsenal. Far from being a gift we grant

to another, it is a boon we bestow upon ourselves. We'll manipulate forgiveness, because ultimately it is ours to give to whomever we desire, under whatever conditions we choose, to achieve whatever ends serve us best.

When I embraced this way of thinking, I didn't realize what I was up to at first. I bounced along those oil-field roads, fuming and fretting, night after night. And all the while I was busy creating a god. From the junkyard of my past, I assembled the scrap metal of self-preservation, self-righteousness, and unalloyed selfishness, then welded together a hollow deity. In its core, I stuffed myself: a god without divinity, offering sinners forgiveness with conditions and without love.

This other myth of forgiveness is a carbon copy of the first. Both the forgiveness we desire from God and the forgiveness we extend to others have a multitude of strings attached. Both are conditional, hinging upon human action. "If I do this, then God will do that." Likewise, "If my offender does this, then I will do that." Whether forgiveness happens is ultimately our decision. In this myth we've managed to upend forgiveness completely. We're behind the wheel in the vehicle of absolution—that's what we assume, anyway. But, thanks be to God, it's all an illusion. That's the good news to come. So bear with me, because before we get there, we should take a good look at the last myth: the necessity of forgiving ourselves.

I remember the weekend well. I'd gotten some pizza with a friend. Afterward we went to her place and kicked back on her front porch. Some neighborhood kids were laughing as they ran through a sprinkler. An old couple walked by on their evening stroll. She went back inside, brought out a couple of beers, and we started swapping stories from our past. Years before, she had gone through her own hell of shame and guilt. An affair. An unwanted pregnancy. Dreams that never came true. She seemed a sympathetic listener, so I opened up a bit about my own story. I described how I felt: like my past was a stalker I couldn't escape, a ghost haunting me with accusations everywhere I went. She heard me out, then put her finger on what seemed to be my fundamental problem. "God has forgiven you, Chad. Now you need to forgive yourself." I sat there in silence for a minute. Then I looked at her and said, "You know, all this time, I've never thought about it like that. I think you may be on to something."

Forgive myself. Maybe that was my problem and my solution all in one. All these hang-ups I had about whether God had forgiven me, all the conditions I had concocted serving as a basis for divine absolution—all of that was ultimately a side issue. What was really holding me back was my refusal to forgive myself.

At some point in your life, you've probably received—or given—the same advice my friend gave me. What does it matter if others have forgiven me, if even God himself has forgiven me, if I'm still withholding forgiveness from myself? So you screwed up your marriage and now find yourself divorced and lonely; it's time to forgive yourself for your mistakes and move on. So you messed up as a parent and blame every mistake your child now makes on the mistakes you made as a mom or dad. Look, we all make mistakes. Just accept that we can't do anything to alter our past failures. What's done is done. Let go of the guilt. Get out of the past. It's time to break the chains of blame. You deserve freedom. Everyone does.

Until self-forgiveness breaks through, the stalker will prowl about our world, spewing forth words of accusation. Only when we forgive ourselves will this haunting ghost of guilt finally vanish for good.

I swallowed this myth whole—hook, line, and sinker. God had done his part; now it was up to me to do mine. I'd meet God halfway, or at least partway. He had supplied 95 percent of the forgiveness, and by forgiving myself, I would supply the other 5 percent. If I did that, I'd be okay again. A full and perfect forgiveness would be mine. I'd finally grasp that elusive peace, and my conscience could rest.

It took me a while, but I gradually realized what I was doing. I had made myself the human tail wagging the divine dog. I had elevated myself to the status of ultimate forgiver. I correctly diagnosed the problem—I still struggled with guilt and shame—but the solution I accepted was a wrong turn. As with the other delusions, I made myself the axis around which absolution rotated.

THESE THREE MYTHS about forgiveness are, in reality, just one myth with three facets: one in relation to God, another in relation to others, and the third in relation to ourselves. What unites them is egocentricity. Just as our egos lead to our downfalls, so even in the aftermath, our egos block the way to restoration. We are unwilling to let God be God. If there is any forgiving to be done, we want to earn it, grant it to others, and self-give it. So twisted is the self upon the self it even hijacks forgiveness from the Father to force it to serve its own ends.

Only by the grace of God in Christ did a wrecking ball fall from heaven to demolish the edifice I had constructed on these myths. What I realized then was that no strings are attached to the forgiveness God gives us in his Son. We can't "buy" it by being sorry. We can't guarantee ongoing forgiveness by living obediently. And we can't sin our way out of forgiveness once God has bestowed it. Forgiveness is taken entirely out of our hands and placed in the hands of the Savior whose scars tell the story of unconditional love.

Even before we knew we needed it, desired it, or thought we could do the slightest thing to earn it, God gave it in full. We weren't the friends of God or even strangers to him when he reconciled us to himself; we were his adversaries.[2] As author Kimm Crandall says, "While you were sinning God came after you! While you were still selfishly pursuing your own interests, binging and purging, finding your worth in your work, cutting your own body, using people for sex, indulging in pornography, overeating, abusing alcohol, turning over to drug addiction, and giving God and the rest of the world a cantankerous kiss-off, he was stubbornly seeking to redeem you."[3] Yes, while we were still cheating on our spouses, lying to our parents, and not giving a damn about anyone but ourselves, Jesus took our cheating, lying, murdering, and narcissism onto himself and emptied his veins to atone for it all.

Bellying up to the pigs' feed trough alongside that lost and broken son, Christ bridged the gap between us and the Father. To the world he spoke his absolution, earned hanging on the cross: "Father, forgive them, for they know not what they do."[4]

In the parable of the prodigal, the father had forgiven his son long before his child decided to make the journey home. He ran toward the prodigal with the absolution dancing upon his lips. "But while he was still a long way off, his father saw him and felt compassion, and ran and embraced him and kissed him."[5] Let every one of these verbs be written in gold: *saw, felt, ran, embraced, kissed.* All this he did before his son could even speak. And when his son does begin stuttering his rehearsed confession, the father shuts him up halfway through. He doesn't even acknowledge the words his son speaks. As Timothy Keller writes, "Jesus shows the father pouncing on his son in love not only before he has a chance to clean up his life and evidence a change of heart, but even before he can recite his repentance speech. Nothing, not even abject contrition, merits the favor of God. The Father's love and acceptance are absolutely free."[9] The prodigal's father simply calls for the party of the century to begin.

The forgiveness of the Father doesn't wait for us to

demonstrate adequate, sincere repentance. It doesn't let us humbly accept a servant position in the household, or a chance gradually to earn our Father's favor again through a life of obedience. Christ's forgiveness precedes our repentance—and calls it forth.

WE, AND YET NOT WE, FORGIVE. The forgiveness we speak to another person is our own and yet not our own, for it comes only from Christ. Our lips say, "I forgive you," but those words originated upon the lips of Jesus. Once more, we lose control. And in loss is freedom. At the foot of the cross we are equal—equally guilty, equally forgiven, equally loved.

Forgiveness, like life itself, doesn't have our name scrawled on it. It isn't our property, much less our tool or weapon. Those who sin against us don't owe us an apology. They don't owe us repentance, tears, promises of improvement, vows never to repeat what they've done. Nothing is what they owe. When we forgive, we are pressing into the palm of a fellow transgressor the coin of freedom with which Christ has enriched us. We give only what we first received. When the Spirit reveals this to us, we discover what a joy it is to bury the hatchet in an unmarked grave.

In the same grave we bury the myth of self-forgiveness. We're seeking relief from our guilt in the last place we should be looking: ourselves. Forgiveness, like medicine, comes from outside of you, from the hand of a healer. When God forgives us in Christ, he forgives completely. There is no deficiency. Even if, heaven forbid, others refuse to forgive us, we rest peacefully in the only declaration of release that ultimately matters: the one Jesus himself gives from his ugly cross of beautiful love.

In forgiveness we lose the control we thought we had, because there is no controlling the unrelenting, radical grace of a forgiveness-crazy Father. This love is frightening to the careful, reprehensible to the legalist, dangerous to the moralist. But if you've experienced it, you know it's like being yanked out of the grave and having your coffin lid pried open. It is the most unexpected pleasure in the world to be loved without condition by a God who makes no demands.

CHAPTER FIVE

The Struggle to Un-Love Ex-Sins

I HAVE ZERO EXPERIENCE with what many Christians call "the victorious Christian life." I've never made huge strides in holiness, never seen my sanctification level skyrocket, never trampled sin after sin underfoot. If such triumphant believers exist, they're a breed of Christian unicorn we'll never discover because they don't go around bragging about it. Swaggering about growth in sanctification is like boasting of humility.

The truth is, there's an ongoing civil war raging within us. The Apostle Paul describes this daily battle in his letter to the church in Rome. Though writing in the first person, he speaks for all of us: "I do not understand my own actions. For I do not do what I want, but I do the very thing I hate."[1] Paul isn't exaggerating to make a point. He's being brutally honest. This apostle, church-planter, and preacher does the very thing he doesn't want to do. Though he and we are believers, evils still lurk within us. We have "the desire to do what is right, but not the ability to carry it out."[2] So time and again, we lament with Paul, "For I do not do the good I want, but the evil I do not want is what I keep on doing."[3] As Frederick Buechner wrote, "In the whole Bible there are perhaps no words that everybody, everywhere, can identify with more fully" than these.[4]

It should come as no surprise that we find ourselves bloody and bruised on many a battlefield. One day we feel like we're moving forward, and the next as if we've stumbled, fallen backward, and plummeted off a cliff. After weeks or months of sobriety, we decide to have just one drink. And the next thing you know, we're passing cash across the counter and walking out of the liquor store with a heavy sack in our hand. After a workweek from hell, we're craving the narcotic bliss that helps us kiss reality good-bye for a day or two. So we make the call. It doesn't take much: a nostalgic song on the radio, a fight with our spouse, a wink at work, a text from the ex, a bill we can't pay, or simply a daydream we habitually revisit. And all too soon, we're swaggering down our old, self-destructive paths.

We're also citizens of a world fractured by evil and populated by fellow sinners, where the proverbial rug gets ripped right out from underneath our feet. We may be making all the right decisions, only to discover the selfish decisions of others have dismantled the foundation of the life we were endeavoring to rebuild. The gambling addict who's been in therapy and, by the grace of God, has avoided his former way of life—he comes home one day to find his wife has left him for the neighbor down the street. The pastor who's admitted to substance abuse, faithfully attended AA meetings, and stayed on the wagon for months—he finds himself ousted from his church because a disgruntled group of congregational members have orchestrated his dismissal. Often, in the aftermath of these losses, the darkness of our past returns with a vengeance. Old wounds begin to bleed again.

Most sinister of all, we feel deceived by hope, tricked by God. God walked with us through everything: He pulled us away from decorating the darkness, led us to accept the blame for our former sins, revealed himself as the one hidden in our suffering, and received us as his forgiven and forgiving children. Certain we're on the pathway to healing, we suddenly discover this road has led us on a circular route where we once again meet ourselves crouched amidst the ruins of our life.

What the hell is going on?

I'D RATHER NOT REVEAL more about how messed up my life became. I don't want to describe the painful, embarrassing setbacks I experienced. I have no desire to translate into words the indescribable rage I felt against heaven when I became convinced God was a Grand Deceiver.

But because the church has often swallowed whole the language of "the victorious Christian life" without addressing the struggles believers face, I'll revisit this part of my past.

"The victorious Christian life" is, quite frankly, a fairytale version of a life no one actually lives. We fail and fall and question if we'll ever get up. We leave the pigsty with the prodigal son only, six months later, to find ourselves knee-deep in the mud again. Let's begin with Paul's insistence that, far too often, "I do the very thing I hate."[5] Let's talk about doing things we hate, as well as having things done to us we hate. Let's also do it with this goal in mind: as fellow pilgrims in spiritual battle, to meet Paul where he cries out in anguish: "Wretched man that I am! Who will deliver me from this body of death?"[6]

What may appear to others as a trifling detail in daily life can be pregnant with deep meaning. I remember such a momentous detail on my own journey a few years ago. It was March of 2010. I was standing in the hallway of my two-bedroom rental house. It was late, and I was bone-tired from an exhausting day of work. But before I crawled into bed, I walked to the back door. I reached out, smiled a knowing smile, and for the first time in a long time, turned the latch to lock the door.

A trifling detail? Not to me. The simple turning of that lock signified a greater turning occurring in my life. For the four years prior to that time, I didn't care much if I lived or died. In fact, when I did pray, I often asked God to end my life. I left my doors unlocked at night, daring an intruder to sneak in and finish me off as I slept. I was convinced that death would be a godsend. I erected few barriers between myself and the grave—an attractive alternative to the pointless life I was enduring. I was bankrupt of hope.

To deny the bankruptcy, I took up running. I ran marathons and other long-distance races, with every sweat-drenched mile releasing feel-good endorphins that faded all too quickly. I chased hope down to the bottom of countless bottles of Jim Beam. Each one granted a numbing stupor that too soon subsided. Desperate for hope, I looked to the beds of various women. But I couldn't run or drink or sex my way free from the clutches of despair. I needed something, someone, to give me more than temporary euphoria. I needed stability, longevity, a hope anchored in a future worth living. That's when I met her.

FINALLY, I WAS CONVINCED I had awoken to spring after an interminable winter. She was an answer to my prayers. But more than that: I began to view her as the embodiment of God's guarantee that he didn't hate me, that he hadn't given up on me, that I indeed had a future and a hope. I felt like a modern-day Lazarus; I danced out of my tomb, an astonished smile beaming from my face.

We met, we dated, and, after a rapid courtship, we stood side-by-side in front of the altar. With this new marriage, other new gifts arrived on my doorstep. I landed a job outside the oil field, with a freight company. I had better hours and higher pay. My wife and I purchased a lovely home together, in a nearby town, where we could both make a fresh start. She had two young children, as did I, so we began the process of intertwining our separate lives into a united family. I was a husband again. I was also a stepfather. It seemed I was on my way to being whole again. I felt free, hopeful, and happy for the first time in years.

And every night, in a personal ritual that relived the

night of hope reborn, I made sure all the doors in our home were locked.

In that same home, however, late one winter afternoon, all the locks in the world couldn't bar the entrance of hope's demise. Sitting across from me in the kitchen, my wife, a mere seven months after we'd stood at the altar and said "I do," looked up and said, "I don't love you."

Nothing catastrophic had precipitated this declaration. We had faced the normal obstacles newly married couples encounter when integrating two lives. But she concluded that, in our case, these obstacles were ultimately insurmountable. She wanted out. She said she would be filing for divorce that week—and she did. As if a dark comedy laughed in the face of human tragedy, snow and freezing rain smothered our town that night.

Four years after I sat alone on an apartment floor, wanting nothing more than to die, I sat alone on the floor of our empty house. In darkness. In despair. In the ruins of a life once more destroyed.

MOST OF US, at some point in our lives, experience the shock of watching the very thing we waited so long to attain slip through our fingers. Major and minor setbacks will come. They're inevitable. When they happen, worldly wisdom advises us to pick up the pieces and start fresh. When life hands you lemons, make lemonade. What doesn't kill you makes you stronger. Crack open any fortune cookie, and you'll find these and other hollow proverbs inside.

They all boil down to one assumption: we are capable of redeeming our lives, no matter how bad things become.

This notion is attractive. It affirms an ability within us to bring any Goliath down to his knees. It's an optimistic view of the unconquerable human spirit. It urges us, despite our losses spinning in a tornadic chaos, to declare we're okay. We will overcome. Past our surface weaknesses, we're promised we'll see a purer, stronger version of who we are. When setbacks occur, this inner strength becomes the reservoir on which we rely.

But this reservoir turns out to be a mirage. If we try to slake our thirst there, we'll wind up with a mouthful of sand. When setbacks befall us, the more inward we turn, the more we look to ourselves as the fixer and redeemer of our broken situations—and the worse things will become, especially if they get better first.

When, on the surface, we appear to have fixed our problems, patched up the holes in our deflated lives, then the lie with which we began waxes stronger. Accomplishments provide temporary comfort in the form of self-affirmation and pave the way for more disastrous losses to come. In the end, the worst thing that can happen to us when we've experienced a major setback in our lives is successfully to overcome it on our own. Top-heavy with pride, we're even more prone to wind up flat on our face.

So there I was. A second wife gone. Another divorce scarring my life. Heavy waves of shame and humiliation, anger and bitterness rolling over me. I moved out of the house and rented a cheap duplex for my new home. An interstate roared a block away as rage roared within me. I was uncertain about many things, but of one thing I was completely confident: God had lied to me about hope, lied to me about a fresh chance at life, lied to me about a future bright with happiness.

In a sadistic desire to see me hurt again, God had deceived me even more deeply this time. He was not love. Nor was he hate. Either one of those would mean he actually cared. No, he was a powerful being who, out of boredom or apathy or fickleness or meanness, toyed with human lives. And if that meant luring us into hope, he would do it. And then he'd walk away, laughing.

God turned his back on me, so I turned my back on

him. Since he didn't care about my marriage, I didn't care about anyone else's marriage, either. Nothing really mattered except surviving another day. Eat, drink, and be merry—or fake it at least—for tomorrow you may die. Don't trust God ever again, I told myself. In fact, don't trust anyone. Keep them all at arm's length. Do whatever feels good, whatever will get you through this day, this night, this week. You'll make it through this eventually. It might take a while, but you will. And when you do, you can look back and boast, "I showed everyone—including God—I didn't need them. I'm a survivor."

When we believe this lie, the real tragedy is what we become. We do the very things we hate. We walk down those paths leading us to deeper darkness and destruction, to places where our ex-sins look like salvation. We fool ourselves into thinking that, thanks to our resolve, our will to survive, we have weathered this storm. No thanks to God, we have managed to piece together our broken lives again. But sooner or later, the truth of our predicament will emerge. Our entire existence is governed by a pantheon of fake gods, chief among them our own ego.

JEREMIAH DIAGNOSED OUR AILMENT long ago: "The heart is deceitful above all things, and desperately sick; who can understand it?"[7] If our hearts were only deceitful or only desperately sick, that would be tragic enough. But the alliance of the two is deadly. The Hebrew word for "deceitful" is the same root in the name of that devious patriarch Jacob, whose life is punctuated with grasping, self-serving lies. The Hebrew word for "desperately sick" is better translated as "beyond remedy" or "incurable." It describes hearts not merely afflicted with clogged arteries in need of a spiritual stent or two. There's no plumbing the depths to which our hearts have fallen.

None of us like this unflattering description of ourselves. We spend most of our lives in an ongoing state of denial about our true condition. We're like chain-smoking couch potatoes who keep boasting about the upcoming marathons we'll run. The deceitful heart achieves that goal easily. It is, as John Calvin described it, "a perpetual factory of idols."[8] It churns out the pseudo-gods we look to for help or escape. They may be anything from drugs to sex, money to power, family to church. The dark surprise here is that they may not all be bad things—some of them may be good. (It's the adoration we pay them, the trust we have in them, that transforms them into self-made gods.)

To realize the heart of our problem is also to realize

the heart of God's solution. But it's not what we might first imagine. We might suppose that our Lord, seeing us struggle with false worship and its manifold fruits in our life, pumps strength into our hearts so we fight free of our attachment to lies. Or that he's like a life coach who teaches us how to rid ourselves of hurtful practices so we can begin to live to his glory.

The fatal flaw? Both these views of how God works are only slight amendments of the fiction that we're capable of redeeming our lives, no matter how bad things become. All that's different is we've added "with God's help." With God's help, we will overcome our hearts. With God's help, we will conquer our obstacles. With God's help, we will redeem any tragedy our lives become.

God, however, is not here to help us. He is not our assistant, our coach, or our motivator. He is here to do for us what we cannot, and will not, do for ourselves. Part of how he does this is by launching a full-scale assault against the temple of our hearts. The exact form of this attack varies from person to person. But rest assured of one thing: it will hurt. God's destruction of our false deities will leave us bitter, likely bewildered, and always ready to fight God to get our god(s) back. This is no playground spat between two rivals. This is the Lord of heaven and earth warring with the deeply entrenched evil within us.

THIS INTERNAL WAR frequently gets quite messy. In fact, it often appears as if the opposite of what God desires is occurring. Looking back at my own life, I can trace the path of my undoing. I divinized my second wife. I would sooner have lost God than lost her. I also worshiped the "life" I'd newly created. It, not God, was the source of my joy. It, not God, was what I trusted to get me through the day. My salvation was a new marriage, and my hope was this newfound family that I was smart enough, handsome enough, and lucky enough to make my own. So I had fallen back into my old ways, into believing that I was the creator of my own life. Instead of un-loving ex-sins, I had once more embraced a life in which I was the center, not God.

When God made use of my wife's abandonment of our marriage to wage war against this self-serving worship within me, I became angry, bitter, and convinced that God was a liar. I went back to my old ways, stubbornly rebelling against him. If God said, "Thou shalt not," I thought, "By God, I will." I was furious over his stripping away of my destructive attachments to lies. How dare he attack my favorite falsehoods! So I waged a war of my own against God—the war of a dying man, dying to the lies that were my own undoing. And, yes, things got quite messy for a while.

What God was doing with me is what he does with all of us: redeeming our lives by killing the death within us. He is not there to assist us in this destruction and reconstruction. He is there to do it all himself, all for us. And despite what we might assume, his sole motivation for doing so is grace and mercy.

Remember what Paul says, after lamenting the struggles he and we face? "Wretched man that I am! Who will deliver me from this body of death?" he asks.[9] Here's his answer: "Thanks be to God through Jesus Christ our Lord!" Thanks be to God, for in Christ alone does the truth of God's work in our lives become clear. He doesn't empower us to live a life that will ultimately please him. He doesn't lend us a hand as we fight free from the clutches of idolatry. He doesn't show us the way to refine our hearts so we might love him alone. Jesus *accomplishes for us* everything the Father desires, despite our selfish attempts to thwart his work every step of the way.

OVER TIME I CAME TO DISCOVER that the real victorious life is found in a place that looks like defeat. It's a messy place, full of pain and loss and lots of blood. It's the acre of soil where we stand and look up at the God who, like a sponge, absorbed all our defeats and self-destructive ways. If you want a job done right, do it yourself. So that's what God did. He fought and won the fight we could never win. All the ex-sins we struggle to un-love are undone on his cross of love.

Then why are things still so hard? Why are we so embittered when our Father rids us of our self-delusions and lies? Why do we so often find ourselves bloody and bruised on the battlefields of this life? Because every day of this life is a day to relearn who we really are in the eyes of God.

Our Father rewrites our life stories with the ink of the cross. He takes our botched narratives full of self and fills them with Jesus. "My Son," he says, "is now who you are. He is your story, your identity, your everything." You might say that we have experienced the only good kind of identity theft. Jesus has stolen away our old identity and given us a new one. He became who we were, and we become who he is.

Even on our darkest days, when we sit in empty houses full of broken dreams, when we fight with the demons of past failures, who we really are remains unchanged. We are the forgiven. We are those bought back. We are those embraced by a Father who, not for a single moment, even on our worst days, will stop loving us.

CHAPTER SIX

The Glorious Freedom of Vulnerability

W HEN I WALKED into the farmhouse, he was sitting at his kitchen table, dressed in his customary overalls. The family's King James Bible was open in front of him. Elmer Krieg usually greeted me with a smile and a handshake. Today he just waved me over to the table and told me to have a seat. His elderly face was a theatre of emotion: shock, dismay, disgust. I didn't know what was wrong, but clearly something was troubling him. So I sat down across from him and waited for him to deliver the bad news.

Since Elmer had multiple health issues, I assumed that he'd received an unfavorable report from the doctor that week.

"No," he said, shaking his head.

"Your grandchildren okay?"

"Oh, yes, they're fine."

"Then what's up?"

He looked down at the Bible and tapped it repeatedly, almost accusingly. "This," he said, "is what's wrong." I'm sure I looked confused. So he opened it to Genesis, paged over a few chapters, and said, "Listen to this." I sat silently as he began to read. When he finished, Elmer looked up, met my eyes, and said, "I can't believe *that's* in the Bible."

In all Elmer's eighty-plus years—all those years of Sunday school, church services, and home devotions— somehow he'd managed to skip over one of the most odious stories of Scripture. What he read to me was the account of what happened to Lot and his daughters after the Lord reduced their hometown of Sodom to ashes.[1] He'd never heard that the family of three went into hiding in a mountain cave, that the daughters got Lot drunk on two successive nights, had intercourse with their father, and both wound up bearing sons from this incestuous union.

That this shameful narrative was actually recorded on the pages of the Holy Bible had sent Elmer into a tailspin. He was upset, scandalized. At that moment, he became my teacher. He showed me how easy it is for churchgoers to miss one of the most glaringly obvious truths about the Scriptures: they contain not the spotless biographies of saints but the soiled résumés of sinners.

THAT'S ONE OF THE MOST REMARKABLE features of the biblical narrative—and one of the most instructive. No attempt is made to clean up embarrassing episodes from the lives of God's people. In fact, the Scriptures seem to go out of their way to highlight the infamous stories of famous believers. Lot, for instance, though he is called "righteous" three times by Peter, has a string of unrighteous marks against him.[2] He had to separate from his Uncle Abraham because of disputes between their herdsmen.[3] He foolishly chose to settle his family in Sodom, even though his neighbors were "wicked, great sinners against the LORD."[4] He offered his virgin daughters to a rape-hungry mob when they threatened to attack Lot's two guests.[5] When the angels warned him that God was about to destroy his hometown, he dragged his feet instead of fleeing.[6] And, as we read in the final scene recorded about him, he was a drunk, naked father having sex with his daughters. Lot was a righteous man who couldn't seem to do anything right. No wonder Elmer tapped his Bible with an accusing finger.

Why, in the line strung from Genesis to Revelation,

is so much dirty laundry hanging there for all the world to see?

To get to the answer to that question, let's imagine for a moment a very different Bible—the Scriptures rewritten so that the failures of God's people are expunged from the record. Suppose Adam and Eve didn't spit out God's command and devour the forbidden fruit. Suppose Noah didn't get wasted on wine and pass out in his tent. Joseph's brothers didn't stab him in the back. Judah didn't hire his daughter-in-law as a prostitute and impregnate her. Moses didn't lose his temper and strike the stone. Aaron didn't mold the idolatrous calf. David didn't bed Bathsheba and knock off her husband. What message would this heavily edited version of the Bible send?

The message it would send about the Old Testament people is the same message we want to believe about ourselves: that the spiritual life is about being strong, not weak; victorious, not defeated; standing tall, not humbled low. This rewritten Bible would affirm the widespread delusion that the masks of strength we wear in public are part of the God-pleasing, standard-issue uniform of the faithful.

WE LOVE MASKS, which conceal our true identity with a fabricated one. When we habitually wear them, we forget we even have them on. Our fabricated face becomes the way we present ourselves to the world, to the church, to our family, to ourselves, and even to God. In fact, it becomes so much a part of our identity that we assume it's who we really are. It's the part of us that author Kimm Crandall calls "the imposter," which spends "years building an identity worthy of other people's approval."[7] This imposter becomes the basis on which we seek affirmation and acceptance from others.

To cover our weaknesses, we wear the mask of strength. To cover our unfaithfulness, we wear the mask of fidelity. To cover our doubts, we wear the mask of bold assertions. To cover our pride, we wear the mask of humility.

But we forget a critical feature of masks: they not only conceal but reveal. What they reveal is our greatest fear: that others, including God, will discover who we really are. But as theologian Steven Hein reminds us, *"You cannot meet God as He truly is until you have met up with yourself as you really are."*[8] And that means being unmasked.

Of all the struggles we face on the long, crooked road of repentance, this fear of exposure is perhaps the most pervasive. And the most persuasive. It dogs us every step of the journey. Whether we're happily married or on the cusp of divorce, watching our children graduate *magna cum laude* or bailing them out of jail, landing our dream job or filing for unemployment benefits, we have masks for different occasions—good, bad, or in between—to cover up our true condition.

With our mask-wearing proclivity ever-present, removing those masks seems counterintuitive to both common sense and religious sensibilities. We have a deep-seated aversion to naked honesty, inside and outside the walls of religious institutions. As author Rachel Held Evans observes, "We think church is for taking spiritual Instagrams and putting on our best performances."[9] Common sense tells us to fake strength lest others spy our weakness, to boast of our best, not our worst. Religious sensibilities echo this. Don't admit you often doubt God's goodness or existence. Admit, in generic terms, that you too are a sinner (that's expected and permissible), but never specify which sins are yours (that makes you seem weak). "The pious fellowship permits no one to be a sinner," Dietrich Bonhoeffer wrote. "So everyone must conceal sin from himself and from the fellowship. We dare not be sinners. Many Christians are unthinkably horrified when a real sinner is suddenly discovered among the righteous. So we remain alone in our sin, living lies and hypocrisy."[10]

Consider this: Isn't our constant wearing of masks deceptive, exhausting, and enslaving? As frightening as the removal of these masks may be, it is a divine act of gracious liberation in which Christ _frees us to be weak._

A MONTH AFTER MY SECOND DIVORCE was finalized, I received one of those phone calls you never forget. I was sitting in my truck on a hot summer day in the west Texas town of Lubbock. My children's stepfather was on the line. He was calling to tell me that he had accepted a job offer near San Antonio, Texas. My children, who had been living less than an hour away from me, would soon be moving eight hours away. They would relocate to a new town, study at new schools, make new friends. At the end of our polite conversation, I thanked him for letting me know and said good-bye. And for the next several minutes, I sat there with the truck idling, but my mind racing in high gear. What would I do?

It didn't take me long to decide. If my children were moving, then I was moving, too. Moving would also give me the chance to put the town that had been my home in the rearview mirror. Its crisscrossing streets were a cobweb that trapped me in memories. On every corner sat a restaurant or a movie theater that recollected those few happy days before the failure of my second marriage. In San Antonio I could start fresh. Not a soul knew me there—knew my past, knew my failures. I would stuff my belongings into a U-Haul once again. I would meet new friends, avoid old temptations. Here was a golden opportunity to recreate a life for myself that I could be proud of.

We've all had experiences like this. An opportunity opens up to start a new chapter in life, one that seems like it will allow us to pen words of success instead of defeat. Maybe it's a breakup or a divorce, a stint in rehab, a recovery from bankruptcy, or simply an escape from circumstances in which life seemed trapped in the vortex of failure. Most of us see that as a chance to turn over a new leaf.

This can be good—it can be just the opportunity we need. But it can also be an opportunity fraught with danger. It can foster the very environment conducive to a recreated life that is opposite of God's desires for us—one in which we keep right on wearing the same old worn-out masks of self-generated, self-serving strength.

When I boxed up my belongings for the move to San Antonio, I left a few things behind. An old recliner. Some cheap bookshelves. But the one thing I should have left behind, I carefully packed and loaded onto the truck: my collection of disguises. The new setting seemed a perfect opportunity to wear them.

No one knew me there. So I could put on the mask of strength without anyone realizing how weak I had been, and still was. I could pretend to be a truth-teller without anyone realizing how prone to lying I had been, and still was. I could even find a congregation and act the part of a pious churchgoer without anyone realizing the moral failures that marred my past, and against which I still struggled. I told myself that in this new place I could remake a life that I could be proud of. But in fact, all I was doing was covering up my old life with recycled masks. This is the hazard of a pseudo-life.

OUTWARD CIRCUMSTANCES do not alter our inner dispositions. The horde of selfish cravings swarming within us do not respect boundaries; they travel with us wherever we go, whoever we're around, whatever job we have. I'm reminded of the story of Jerome, the fourth-century church father. To escape the allure of lust, he moved to a desert monastery. Yet even there, far removed from the opposite sex, his mind was still filled with visions of scantily clad dancing girls. Though he relocated to what he thought was a safe place, Jerome could not escape Jerome.

We like to think the issue is the bottle or the pill or the casino; the attractive next-door neighbor or the porn site; the applause of the crowd or the next rung on the ladder. But we're just like Jerome, blinded by these allurements to the real issue. We can't escape our problem because it's not external to us. It is *within* us.

Wearing a mask of spirituality or moral improvement is deceptive because it perpetuates the delusion that we can fix ourselves. It's also exhausting because we must be ever-vigilant to keep up appearances. Along with deception and exhaustion comes enslavement. As long as the masks are in place, we lie to God, others, and ourselves. We wear ourselves out by pretenses of self-improvement. And the walls of our captivity to a fictitious life keep closing in. It all makes for a perfect storm of self-destruction. That's why all these lies often lead to depression, self-loathing, and despair. There's nothing more crippling in life than the refusal to admit who we are for fear of being rejected by the very confession of our identity.

To return to the opening words of this chapter, that's precisely why the Scriptures document the downfalls of believers. The Bible unmasks the stories of men and women to reveal their true, sin-laden identities. Because of that, we are able to see ourselves in them:

- We are Adams and Eves: the covetous desire to consume that which God has forbidden lures us into acts that fill us with shame.
- We are Noahs: even after the Lord has rescued us from threatening perils, we misuse God's gifts in creation to become intoxicated with the pleasures of the flesh.
- We are Abrahams and Isaacs: in a selfish desire to save our own skin, we resort to lies that endanger those closest to us.
- We are Davids: lust lures us into adulteries of the heart, if not of the body.

We are all of these—and more.

THE BIBLE IS THE RECORD of men and women who struggled against—and often succumbed to—the same temptations we meet. It is as much the story of accountants, pastors, and stay-at-home moms as it is the story of patriarchs, prophets, and kings. As they are unmasked, so are we.

More importantly, we read the stories of how God revealed their vulnerabilities, and we see why God did it. He was at work in their lives to reveal not how strong they were, but how very weak. Through those stories, he opens our eyes not to some hidden reservoir of integrity within us, but to the swamp of vice inside us all. He doesn't lead us into temptation, but he uses temptation to reveal our desire to give in to it.

This is the crucial difference between us and God. We want a life free of sins, burdens, and weaknesses. But God uses these very things to show us that freedom comes when the Lord brings us to the point of admitting our bondage, our weakness. And that there's not a single thing we can do now or in the future to muscle our way to liberation and victory.

Paul gives us an example from his own life to illustrate the counterintuitive way that God works. The apostle was in danger of succumbing to pride because he had received grand revelations from the Lord, celestial visions of unspeakable grandeur.[11] He was caught up to the third heaven, into paradise, and "heard things that cannot be told, which man may not utter."[12] These experiences, as full of wonder as they were, could easily have filled Paul with hubris. "Look at me," he might have thought. "I'm a cut above the rest. As reward for my obedience, God has exalted me to the third heaven." To prevent Paul from ballooning out in pride, the Lord popped his bubble with a sharp thorn. "So to keep me from becoming conceited because of the surpassing greatness of the revelations," Paul tells us, "a thorn was given me in the flesh, a messenger of Satan to harass me, to keep me from becoming conceited."[13]

Exactly what this thorn was, we don't know. What we do know is that Paul wanted it removed. It was a cross he didn't want to bear, a weakness that stifled the strength he wanted to exhibit. So he prayed that God would extract the thorn, remove the impediment that prevented him from being the strong man he wanted to be. But God said No. When Paul repeated his plea, the Lord said No again. "Three times I pleaded with the Lord about this," Paul wrote, "that it should leave me."[14]

How can we not sympathize with Paul? We not only feel his frustration—we *live* it. How are we supposed to stand on our own two feet when situations in life always seem to cripple us in some way? We have asked God to remove temptations from our life, but they remain as unwelcome hindrances. We have asked him to drive away the torments from our past sins, but they still afflict us. How can we be strong when weakness is our constant companion? How can we be self-sufficient when we must constantly look outside ourselves for help?

To us the Lord says what he said to Paul: "My grace is sufficient for you, for my power is made perfect in weakness."[15] Here is the light of revelation that dispels the darkness of our delusions. Jesus is not making us weak. Rather, he wants us to realize that we already *are* weak. The thorns, crosses, messengers of Satan—call them what you will—are themselves the means of revelation.

Through them the Spirit opens our eyes to see who we truly are. We realize, in our weakness, that we are totally dependent on the strength that comes from the grace of Christ. Jesus's undeserved love is not one of the things we need; it is the one thing needful. The thorns in our flesh unmask us, as we begin to realize we have everything we need in him.

I LEARNED THIS LIBERATING TRUTH the hard way. Most of us do. I had supposed that a fresh start in San Antonio would be just the reboot my life needed. But while my outward circumstances had changed, my inner weaknesses had not. I was still me. I had a new job, fostered new friendships, even found a new church, but I was not a new person.

Lured by the same old temptations, I was the same old sinner. But Christ was peeling away the masks that concealed my true identity to reveal my greatest fears. I rebelled. He persisted. Thorns kept pressing into my flesh. And eventually he showed me what he showed Paul: that his grace is sufficient for me, for his power is made perfect in my weakness.

God used my teenage daughter to show me this truth. She was almost eight years old when she and her brother waved good-bye to me as the car drove away the first time. I moved—twice—to where they lived so I could be with them as much as possible during their growing-up years. Still, I had never once spoken to them about what happened between their mom and me. But that day finally came.

On one of the weekends when my children were with me, I noticed my daughter, now fourteen, was fighting back tears as she got ready for bed. I sat down next to her, put my arm around her, and asked what was wrong. For several minutes she didn't utter a word. She just sat there, wiping away tears. Then, as if six years of emotion exploded all at once, she cried out, "Why did you cheat on Mommy?"

The words hit me like a fist to the gut. And I realized, at that moment, I had a choice to make. I could lie. I could say her mom was making stuff up to make me look bad. I could concoct excuses or shift blame, talk about how troubled our marriage was, suggest that her mom had been a bad wife to me. I could downplay my infidelity or use delaying tactics to avoid answering her. In other words, I could hide behind falsehoods, pretend in front of my daughter. Or I could peel away the mask, make myself vulnerable, and tell her the hard, transparent truth.

When I walked out of her room about half an hour later, I felt more free than I had in years. Maybe my entire life. It was a turning point, an epiphany. I had never known the liberating power of weakness until I knelt at the foot of my daughter's bed and told her who I really was. I talked about my pride, my ego, my infidelity. I told her the story I'm telling you now.

I moved to San Antonio hoping for a fresh start. I never dreamed this would be it—that it would come by my being vulnerable before a young child who, at that moment, embodied the love of Jesus for me. She forgave me, embraced me, and the two of us cried together. This is how I learned that freedom comes not from pretending I'm someone I'm not, but from a loving welcome from one who accepts me as I am.

THE GRACE OF CHRIST is enough for all of us: it frees us not only to be sinners in ourselves, but to be saints in him. We don't glory in sin; we confess it. There's no need to pretend otherwise. Instead, there is every need to admit our personal identity. Christ replaces our false masks with his own true face. This unmasked God masks us with himself. From head to toe, heart to soul, we are covered with the righteousness of Jesus. When our Father looks at us, he sees holy ones—saints, not sinners.

The night I talked with my daughter, I began to burn my own masks in the liberating flames of this truth. Later, I would sit on the couch with my son and make the same confession to him. And burn more masks. With the loss of each disguise, I gained more freedom to rest in the identity I have in Jesus.

When we are weak, Christ is strong within us. And his strength is all the strength we need. We have nothing to prove to anyone, because we are fully approved by God in Jesus Christ.[16] Our weakness becomes the testimony of Christ's work in our lives. "We have this treasure [of the light of the Christ] in jars of clay, to show that the surpassing power belongs to God and not to us."[17]

This is the comforting irony of the Christian life: When we are weak, then we are strong.[18] When he spoke about the Messiah, John the Baptist said, "He must increase, but I must decrease."[19] Those seven words sum up the entirety of the work of the Spirit in our lives. He is decreasing us in order to increase us, strengthen us, and deepen us in Jesus Christ.

In him we discover a freedom that is found nowhere else. If the only true God has adopted me as his child, given me his name in baptism, and stands beside me to claim me as his beloved, then why would I need to pretend that I'm something else?

In Christ, the masks are gone. The pretending is over.

CHAPTER SEVEN

When Love Repents Us

IT'S A SUNDAY MORNING in late summer. Early service in a hilltop church overlooking the northern edge of the city I now call home. The sunlight beams through a stained-glass window high above the altar while an organist paints the air with the colors of ancient tunes. I sit alone in the pew, a Johnny-come-lately to this band of believers. I've discovered a sacred serenity here. A true sanctuary. A home away from home.

Maybe you've stumbled upon a haven like this. It might be a church, or it might be anything but a church. Perhaps it's simply a quiet place where, even for a few moments, the accusations of your conscience are hushed, the fog in your mind clears. You may be alone or surrounded by others. But here is respite, however brief, from the burdens you bear.

After we sing a hymn of invocation, the pastor

moves in front of the congregation. "In the name of the Father and of the Son and of the Holy Spirit," he says. "Amen," we reply. These words drip with baptismal water. They bathe, soothe, re-identify us as the Father's children in Christ. His holy name has been traced upon us. All is well. A psalm is read, and we nod in understanding when we hear, "I was glad when they said to me, 'Let us go to the house of the LORD.'"[1] We are indeed glad to be here.

But as in any house, so in this one, gladness is often fleeting. It ebbs and flows. Its retreat on this particular Sunday is swift and decisive. Like two pinholes in a balloon, two words in the liturgy take the air of joy right out of me. Both adverbs. An adverb adds to a verb, my elementary school teachers instructed me. It further defines or refines it, expands or contracts it. It is one thing to love, for instance, and quite another to love halfheartedly or to love wholly. Adverbs can be like icing on the verbal cake—or like a fly trapped on the sugary top. On this Sunday, the adverbs buzz like a pair of grammatical flies.

It happens as we are confessing our sins. We begin, "I, a poor, miserable sinner, confess unto You all my sins and iniquities. . . ." So far, so good. We admit that we deserve punishment because of our offenses. This is true. Yet these words follow: "But I am heartily sorry for them and sincerely repent of them."

Heartily. Sincerely. I've said these words in the confession of sins many times, but today they arrest me. These adverbs rise up as two prosecutorial attorneys who join forces to convict me of perjury. I try to mouth this confession, but I just don't mean it. Not if I'm honest with myself, and with the God to whom I confess.

PICTURE YOURSELF on the witness stand. You face a barrage of questions.

> Why are you sorry?
> Did you really mean it when you said how bad you felt?
> Are you sorry because you did it or because you got caught?
> Are you sorry because you broke God's law or because you're suffering the consequences?
> Are you *heartily* sorry?
> Do you *sincerely* repent?

DEEPER AND DEEPER the questions probe. The more your repentance is sliced and diced and put under the microscope, the more you question yourself. Worse, the more you question, then doubt, the Father's forgiveness.

No good comes when we attempt to diagnose the motivations for repentance. We become engrossed in our contrition, our confession, our reasons for admissions and apologies. Or, if we're the offended party, we demand that the person who has sinned against us be repentant for all and only the right reasons. In so doing, we make repentance a good work that justifies us. And when we do that, all we accomplish is undermining trust in the forgiveness of the Father.

We take down the body of Jesus from the cross and nail in its place the corpse of our confession.

YEARS AGO, I had a lengthy conversation with a woman who'd had two abortions. The first, she said, was at her parents' insistence, when she was a teenager. The second was her own choice, when she was in college. The father of these children was the same man. They'd had a rocky, on-again, off-again dating relationship. He wasn't the man she wanted to marry—certainly not the man with whom she wanted to raise children. By her own account, she'd been a naïve, frightened, selfish young woman. Abortion had seemed the only way out, so she took it. Now, years later, she was haunted by those pregnancies, plagued by guilt. She no longer made any excuses. She confessed her sin. And what she most desired was the comfort of the Father's word of forgiveness.

But there was a problem. At this point in her life, she was happily married and the mother of two young children. She had earned a college degree and launched a successful career. Everything had turned out well for her. In fact, she told me, she was living the life she'd always dreamed of having. And she knew that, had she not gone through with those abortions, her life would be very different. She would never have met the man she married. They would never have had those two children together.

She was caught in an internal tug-of-war between guilt over her past wrongs and happiness over her present blessings. With a mixture of frustration and anguish, she said to me, "I don't know if God will forgive me. Yes, I am sorry for the abortions, but am I *really* sorry enough? I don't feel completely sincere in my confession. And if I can't be sincere, how can I possibly hope that God will forgive me?"

Her struggle is our struggle. And her misconception is our misconception. Quite simply, we assume we're the ones doing all the work of repenting. It's up to us to come to our senses, recognize our sins, turn away from them, be sorry for them, confess them, believe that God forgives us, and never repeat those sins again. Everything boomerangs back to us: our actions, our feelings, our sincerity, our faith.

No wonder our hearts fill with doubts about God's forgiveness. If we're the ones doing the work of repenting, yet are the very sinners whose failed lives brought about the need for repentance, won't we necessarily fail at this endeavor, too? As long as the focus remains on us, assurance of absolution is tenuous at best, and our doubts will always loom large.

WHY DO WE FOCUS on our motivations for contrition? Why do we keep asking ourselves, "Am I heartily sorry? Do I sincerely repent? Or am I only going through the motions?"

Behind the veil of our confused emotions and self-scrutinizing, the age-old internal battle continues. Our sinful nature is on a crusade, and its target conquest is confession. This part of us always usurps control, making us detest dependence on another, addicted to self-interest. In confession it is no different. Even in this act, we rewrite the script and insert ourselves as the central character. We are engaging in substitutionary atonement, only it's the *wrong* kind.

In this version, we stuff our regrets, our admissions of guilt, and our confession into a hollow mannequin and nail that to the cross. We expect God to forgive us for the purity of our confession. As always, we bring things back to ourselves.

That's why we're troubled when we doubt the sincerity of our confession. We're afraid that, if it has flaws, God will not accept our mannequin sacrifice. So we work at being really good at feeling really bad for what we've done. We must sincerely repent of our insincerity.

When he was a young man in the monastery, Martin Luther would accept no consolation because he never felt "sufficiently contrite" (note the adverb!) for his sins.[2] He compares troubled consciences to geese. When they're attacked by hawks, they try to fly, though they would do better to run. When wolves pursue them, they attempt to run, though they'd fare better by flying. Like geese, we try to flee from guilt this way and that. But we only increase our pain and run deeper into enemy territory. Though many spoke God's word of forgiveness to Luther, he was so preoccupied with his own sorrow that he was deaf to the absolution. But finally, hope broke through.

"IF YOU WAIT until you are sufficiently contrite," Luther says, "you will never get to the hearing of gladness."[3] He distinguishes between our contrition and the word of Christ's forgiveness as between earth and heaven. They are worlds apart. "Even though it be the highest and most perfect, contrition is something very tiny in respect to righteousness. It is nothing at all by which to merit something or to make satisfaction."[4] We must, Luther insists, turn attention away from ourselves—our sorrow, our regret, our confession, our repentance—with ears attuned only to the voice of the Father's forgiveness. Each of us must say to our self, "If I have not been perfectly contrite, what is that to me either?"[5] The quest for perfect repentance is a foolish pursuit, driving us back to ourselves, but not to Christ.

FOR FAR TOO LONG, I beat myself up every day because of what I'd done. Deep within the house of my mind, as in a secret chamber, I had a viewing room where I'd slink in, close the door, and watch memories of past sins. It was insanity to do this, but despite all the good I destroyed by my evil, I couldn't manage to break free from the emotional entanglements of past, illicit relationships.

No matter how hard I tried, I couldn't seem to un-love my ex-sins—not completely, not perfectly. So it seemed obvious to me I wasn't really heartily sorry. That put me right back where I started: feeling hopeless, in need of fixing up my life before God would welcome me back.

For Luther the monk, there came a day when a brother's words of forgiveness shattered his inward focus and ushered hope into his life. Eventually the Lord brought me to that same place of peace, where I still relearn daily.

Here's the hard yet simple lesson. Repentance is not a work that we perform, but a gift that Christ gives. It's not an emotion that we stir up within ourselves, but a motion that Christ enacts within us. This motion is always away from us—away from guilt, away from self-devised methods of atonement—and toward Jesus.

Like the shepherd looking for the lost sheep in the parable of Luke 15, Christ trails after us when we go astray. He finds us, puts us atop his shoulders, and rejoices to restore us to the fold. Notice that he is the active one: he seeks, he finds, he brings us back.

It is not so much that we repent as that he repents us.

Do we contribute anything to this? No, not a thing. From beginning to end, repentance is the divine work of compassionate restoration. Lost sheep don't find their way back; they're the object of a search-and-rescue mission. This is repentance: a gift we receive, not a work we do.

SOME CLAIM that the final parable in Luke 15, the Prodigal Son, contradicts the understanding of repentance as God's work alone. No—in fact, it accentuates and exemplifies it. The son isn't repentant when he "comes to himself" while feeding swine in a faraway land.[6] All he realizes is that he's reached the end of his rope. He devises a plan for re-acceptance: he will earn his way back into the family's good graces. He will say to his father, "I am no longer worthy to be called your son. Treat me as one of your hired servants." In other words, he returns on his own terms. He will atone for what he did by relinquishing his place in the family.

But the father will have none of this. The moment he spots his son off in the distance, his heart overflows with compassion. He sprints out to meet him, takes him in his arms, and kisses him. Before the son can finish his rehearsed plea for re-acceptance, his father proclaims, "Bring quickly the best robe, and put it on him, and put a ring on his hand, and shoes on his feet. And bring the fattened calf and kill it, and let us eat and celebrate. For this my son was dead, and is alive again; he was lost, and is found."[8]

This moment of complete acceptance was the moment of repentance. The father's embrace was this son's day of resurrection. The father's love repented and restored him. This parable enacts in narrative form what Paul meant when he wrote to the Romans, "God's kindness is meant to lead you to repentance."[9] Repentance was the father's work, the father's gift, to his wayward son.

HERE'S ANOTHER LESSON I learned: how bad we feel for what we've done, what mixed motives prompt us to confess, just how broken our hearts may (or may not) be: all of this is spiritual quicksand. The Lord's own words—"You are mine. I forgive you"—are solid rock, the foundation of our hope and peace.

The Lord's words of forgiveness remain true no matter how untrue we feel. But what if we aren't even sure whether we have faith, or enough faith, to believe that God forgives us? Even if we are of little faith, or faithless, Christ remains faithful, for he cannot deny himself.[10] To walk away from us as we wrestle with doubts would be to deny who he is: the Savior who has pledged himself to us.

God cannot lie. When he says we are forgiven, it's true. The fact that we believe it adds nothing to the forgiveness. A person might say they believe the sun is shining, but the sun doesn't shine or shine brighter with that admission of truth. Similarly, to say "Amen" to the absolution is to admit the truth of God's forgiveness in Jesus. Faith *receives* forgiveness; it doesn't create it, strengthen it, or complete it. Christ's forgiveness of us lacks nothing. It is the declaration of the unalterable love of the Father for us.

How weak or strong our faith is, how pure or impure our confession is, how sincere or insincere our repentance may be—all of this is beside the point. Christ didn't die and rise *potentially* for us *if* we believe enough, repent enough, improve enough. The only "enough" is Christ. His assurance of "I forgive you" is as certain as his declaration from the cross: "It is finished." His words do what they say.

As I learned these truths, I also learned the act of forgiveness has no conditions, no requirements, no penalties. As Robert Farrar Capon says, "Confession is not a transaction, not a negotiation in order to secure forgiveness; it is the after-the-last gasp of a corpse that finally can afford to admit it's dead and accept resurrection."[11] It's not a transaction, not a contract. It's God alone, moved by love alone, announcing that he has reconciled us to himself in the death of his Son.

For many years, at the heart of my struggle was the belief that such a contract did exist. For instance, if there were any problems with my children, I'd say to myself, "God is telling you that you're still not sorry enough for what you did to your family." Somehow we're convinced that God made a deal with us. If we clean up our act, display sincere sorrow, and keep to the straight and narrow, then the Lord will finally forgive us. But that point never comes.

Peace finally arrives when we realize that God is not at war with us. "Therefore, since we have been justified by faith, we have peace with God through our Lord Jesus Christ."[12] We are free in Jesus. We are unshackled from accusation, guilt, punishment, and anger, as well as the need to pacify God through good behavior and acceptable repentance.

Repentance is, quite simply, a gift that God gives us. He breaks and heals our hearts. He seeks us out and bears us home. This forgiveness is not contractual but cruciform; it is embedded within the cross, in Christ's blood-and-bone sacrifice for us. It is one-way love, one-way forgiveness, the one and only hope we have.

CHAPTER EIGHT

The Community of the Broken

He checks his watch. 10:35 a.m. He starts the car again, shifts it into drive, then slams it back into park again. His hands quiver. It's been weeks since he's darkened a church door. By now they're belting out the opening hymn. He decides, Okay, I'll go in, but I'll sneak into the back pew. Hightail it during the closing song. No handshakes, no "Seems like I've heard of you . . ." introductions. He's a nameless, faceless stranger to these people. And that's the way he wants it. He knows if they find out who he is, there'll be glances by some, frigid stares by others. Knowing this, he only makes it halfway through the service. When worshipers begin to make their way to the altar for the Lord's Supper, his stomach churns, and he hits the back door. As he speeds away, he vows that he won't be back. Damn church, damn God, damn everything.

THAT'S ME. Thirty-six years old. A thin band of pale skin where my wedding ring used to be. My seminary job is history. My clericals are in the dumpster. Every minister I meet I expect to stab me in the back. I try to avoid thinking of Jesus. And as for his church, I loathe it.

There were times I've called the church beautiful, faithful, beloved. And times I've shunned her. She has called me her zealous, faithful pastor, and she's kicked me to the curb—a shameful, unfaithful embarrassment.

When I was young and naïve, I assumed life in the church would flow along like a Hallmark movie: a bit of angst along the way, to be sure, but always a feel-good ending. I memorized swaths of Scripture. I devoured theology. I preached, I taught, I wrote. I would've done almost anything to serve the church. She was my life.

But I really didn't know her then. The fissures had not yet appeared. But they would—and they did. And when they did, I felt blindsided.

OVER THE YEARS I've listened to the stories of countless friends, colleagues, and strangers who've experienced the same shock. Some, like me, once served in the ministry. Along the way they became entangled in sexual sins, admitted to alcohol or drug addiction, or simply crashed and burned after years of brutal infighting in the church. In the aftermath, they found themselves ostracized by their brothers and sisters still in the ministry, as personas non grata in assemblies paying lip service to forgiveness and restoration.

Others, after years of silent suffering, finally admitted to struggling with same-sex attraction. Of those, some were shunned like lepers of immorality. Still others simply walked away, exhausted by legalism, congregational civil wars, or denominations more concerned with bylaws than the gospel.

Some were in a church ruled by a strict bumper-sticker theology: "God said it. I believe it. That settles it." There was no room for their doubts and misgivings, so they drifted away. Others grew tired of listening to sermons that sounded more like speeches at political conventions or moral pep rallies. Or they questioned the male-dominated power structure of the church and were accused of "not knowing their place." Or they simply got tired of a traditionalist congregation where, when they challenged the way things had always been, you'd have thought they attacked the Nicene Creed.

✝ Ask each of these people why they left the church, and they'll probably ask you why the church left them.

A DECADE HAS SLIPPED BY since I snuck into that back pew one Sunday morning, only to speed away. Today, I'm in a far different place. I serve as a lay leader in a congregation, kneel at the altar beside my brothers and sisters in Christ, and receive our Lord's gifts every Sunday from my pastors.

It's the story of this change that I want to tell you, the story of how I understand the church to be both lovely and broken, full of both desirable and undesirable traits. As such, she is a mirror of who I am as well. And I have learned to love this disappointing church.

The ugly side of life in the church often goes unmentioned or, at best, is sanitized and downplayed. In his book *Under the Unpredictable Plant*, Eugene Peterson compares this photo-shopped view of the church's life to pornography: "Parish glamorization is ecclesiastical pornography—taking photographs (skillfully airbrushed) or drawing pictures of congregations that are without spot or wrinkle, the shapes that a few parishes have for a few short years. These provocatively posed pictures are devoid of personal relationships. The pictures excite a lust for domination, for gratification, for uninvolved and impersonal spirituality."[1] But every congregation has its struggles, squabbles, and selfish tendencies. As Peterson says elsewhere, "Every congregation is a congregation of sinners. As if that weren't bad enough, they all have sinners for pastors."[2] And where sinners congregate, there will be no shortage of disappointments.

The biblical story documents the dark side of the church in excruciating detail. It's the narrative of a faithful God married to an unfaithful people. In fact, were it not for the infidelity of the Lord's people, the Bible would be a mighty short book, because most of its pages chronicle problem after problem.

In the book of Genesis, we meet a small gathering of Jacob's twelve sons, where we find polygamy, incest, jealousy, hatred, infighting, betrayal, and murder. Not a stellar beginning. Later, when the Israelites wander in the wilderness for four decades, they're beset by idolatry, lust, rebellion, grumbling, spite, and sacrilege. Nobody comes out clean. And so it continues. In the book of Joshua, the people get lazy and give up before they conquer the entire Promised Land. In Judges, where everyone does what is right in his own eyes, Israel apes its pagan neighbors. The books of Samuel and Kings repeat the same, sad story. They are the annals of idolatrous kings, pagan worship, child sacrifice, and persecution of prophets.

By the time we read from Genesis through Malachi,

we've been disabused of any notions of a spotless, faithful congregation in Israel. The Old Testament church seems a rather un-churchly place.

But what about the New Testament? Don't God's people finally get their act together then? Not even close. Two of Jesus's closest disciples, Peter and Judas, are directly connected to the work and speech of Satan.[3] The initial concord of the church in Acts soon disintegrates into lies about offerings that leave two people dead.[4] Disputes rage over kosher food and how Jewish the church should be.[5] The congregations that Paul established are rocked by schisms over leadership, gospel-denying heresies, and angel worship.[6] In the church at Corinth, one fellow has shacked up with his stepmother.[7] The letters to the seven churches in Revelation strike the same sad note: the church has left its first love, adopted false teachings and teachers, appears alive but is dead, and has become so lukewarm that God is ready to spit it out of his mouth.[8]

From cover to cover, the gathering of believers in the Bible looks little different from a gathering of unbelievers.

YES, THIS IS ONLY PART of the story. Examples of kindness, faithfulness, and self-sacrifice abound among the people of God. Yet oftentimes, the same people who are praised in one story are condemned in another. Abraham may have been a man of faith, but he also lied on two occasions about his wife. Moses was the friend of God, but he also lost his temper and was prevented from entering the Holy Land. David was a man after God's own heart, but he was also a man after the body of another man's wife.

Believers. Sinners and saints, holy and unholy, ugly and beautiful. They were just like their church. And they were just like our church.

There's no need to hide this. In fact, great harm comes from prettying up ecclesiastical history. The pornographic unreality of a church free of deep and abiding flaws creates unrealistic expectations. And it invites the kind of shocked disappointment that makes many people walk away when that faux image is shattered. Better to be honest. Life in the church is life among fellow sinners.

This life will be marred by selfishness, pettiness, pain, and grief. It shouldn't happen, but it will. And it does. So how can you love a congregation that makes you angry, that decorates itself with scandal, that exhibits all the negative qualities of a humanity curved in upon itself? How can you learn to love a disappointing church?

I'll tell you how it happened with me. It began when I finally came to terms with a humbling, sobering fact: the church finds me just as unattractive as I find her.

AS WE READ through the stories of Israel's past, as well as the church's life in the New Testament, what do we see? Through the stories of the rebellion of Adam, the murder of Cain, the idolatry of Aaron, and the stubbornness of Israel, the Spirit shows us *our* rebellion, *our* murder, *our* idolatry, *our* stubbornness. We are Adam. We are Cain. We are Aaron.

These stories aren't only a window into the lives of others—they're a mirror of our own. At first this thought may sicken us. We want to object, "I'm not like them!" But the Spirit insists on the truth. This is a painful, humbling confession, but it is indispensable when it comes to repairing a damaged relationship with the church. The ugliness we see exhibited in congregations is a reflection of the ugliness we find in our own hearts, too.

Pointing out the flaws of the church is like shooting fish in a barrel. Far too easy. In fact, we may take a twisted pleasure in seeing the church embroiled in scandal because it relieves us of the burden of confessing our own guilt. Rather than taking personal respon-

sibility, we transfer our own wrongdoing onto a congregation, the denomination, or its clergy. That's what
I did.

On the day I sped away from that worship service,
damning the church, God, and everything, I was still
deeply submerged in denial. I pointed an accusing finger in every direction but my own. Two years later, it
happened again. I tried to attend services with a congregation that had known me in prior years. What I en-
countered was the welcoming equivalent of the North
Pole.

Were they wrong to treat me—or anyone else—so
coldly? Yes, of course they were. But I focused so much
upon their ugliness that I ignored the fact that my sin
had created the opportunity for this ugliness to shine.

Hear me well. I make no excuses for pastors who
turn their backs on a fellow minister who has had to
leave the ministry for moral failure. I'm not excusing
any type of bigotry embedded within a church. I'm not
justifying any wrong within the church. What I am urg-
ing, however, is recognizing that far too often we use
such behavior within congregations or denominations
as an excuse for turning a blind eye to our own com-
plicity in evil.

Real change happens when we see the flaws in the

church as a reflection of our own flawed hearts—and when we realize that this community of the broken, the undesirable, is precisely the community where Christ is at work to love and to forgive.

SOME OF US ARE PRONE to establish a kind of DMZ between ourselves and the church, thinking that we're self-protecting by setting up this buffer zone—but actually we're only perpetuating the war within us. In *Searching for Sunday*, Rachel Held Evans writes, "At its best, the church functions much like a recovery group, a safe place where a bunch of struggling, imperfect people come together to speak difficult truths to one another."[9] "It ought to be the one place in the world where we don't have to wear masks," as Steve Brown says.[10] In this flawed assembly, in the gathering of our fellow wounded, is the hospital where the Great Physician pours into our wounds the healing medicine of his mercy.

We can choose to go for a long run on Sunday morning, think about God, and call that "church." We can choose to go for a walk in the woods, plug in our headphones, and listen to a religious podcast. But this solo Christianity is self-serving, self-protecting, and ultimately self-destructive. Christ calls us to that place where he has anchored his saving, life-giving gifts. And that is where his flock gathers with a shepherd around his word and bath and meal.

When my children were young, I made up a game called "Things in the Wrong Place." I would send them, for example, to my desk drawer, where they'd find a spatula. They'd take the spatula to the kitchen drawer, where they'd see a pair of socks. Then they'd take the socks to my dresser, where they'd find the next wrongly placed item.

Eventually, after they'd traced all these Things in the Wrong Place to the final location, they'd discover a special prize that I'd bought for them. I'd laugh as I watched them zigzagging through the house, giggling over finding a roll of toilet paper in the refrigerator or some such silliness. We had a blast. It was fun. But it was a child's game.

And it was exactly the opposite of the game God our Father plays with us. God doesn't send us scampering all over his creation, eventually discovering the prize he's purchased for us. He tells us precisely where his gifts are received. No maze to work through, no game of Things in the Wrong Place.

In Eden, the Lord told Adam and Eve they would consume life in the fruit of a specific tree. In Jerusalem, he told the Israelites his home address. They would receive atonement, forgiveness, and cleansing at his temple, where he dwelt between the cherubim. He located himself and his gifts where they could easily be found and received. No searching, no exploring, no game.

AFTER ALL MY YEARS of stubborn rebellion, God brought me back into a community where fellow sinners gather around a forgiving Savior. The scars on my soul are still there. But then, we're not gathered to look good. The church is a healing haven for the sick, the wounded, the dying. Here, in our Father's house, things are in the right place.

At the front of the sanctuary stands a place for baptism. In our tradition, we call it a font. And it's right in the middle of everything—really, as it should be. Like the Red Sea, baptism is a body of water we pass through to get to where the Lord wants us to be. In it he drowns the Egyptian army of sins and shame that hounds us. Pharaoh's chariots lie rusting in the bottom of every font. Unlike the Israelites, however, we don't walk through baptism dry-shod. We get drenched. It's a God-ordained drowning. Scarlet letters sink beneath dark waves. Years of drug abuse perish in those waters. And it is a streaming into Christ himself. "We were buried therefore with him by baptism into death, in order that, just as Christ was raised from the dead by the glory of the Father, we too might walk in newness of life," a life saturated with grace.[11]

In this church is a pulpit. Pulpits often have a bad rap. Think "bully pulpit." But not every one is a platform for fist-pounding and arm-twisting. The word itself has a naval origin, and *pulpit* is another name for the front of a ship. Like a plow, it cuts a furrow through the oceanic field of this world. The pulpit leads us away from our soiled past into the arms of Jesus, in whom we are made clean. The pulpit is there because we need a preacher, a shepherd, who will be the Lord's undershepherd to us. The Lord has always given people to his church for this purpose: prophets, priests, apostles, pastors. Jesus has co-opted their lips as his own. "He who hears you, hears me," he told his disciples.[12] As we hear our pastors proclaim God's word, we hear what the old-timers called *viva vox evangelii*, "the living voice of the gospel."

The high point of every Sunday is the meal, where Jesus gives himself totally to us. No leftovers remain. Like little birds, we open our mouths around the nest of the altar. The body of Jesus, the blood of Jesus, enters our bodies, swims in our veins.

This is a communal meal. Kneeling in an arc around the altar is the rainbow of humanity sharing Christ's life. While I'm there, I like to look around. An octogenarian with a walker. A little girl pretty in pink. A young university know-it-all. What matters here is not our age, race, IQs, or sketchy histories. Nothing matters but the one who feeds us. We are what we eat—the body of Christ—and we radiate his beauty. N. T. Wright says, "When [Jesus] wanted fully to explain what his forthcoming death was all about, he didn't give a theory. He didn't even give [the disciples] a set of scriptural texts. He gave them a meal."[13] The church is never more church than at the altar, where an intimacy from believer to believer, from believers to Jesus, is as thick as blood.

WE'VE ALL SEEN plenty of things in the church that are disappointing. But Christ and his church are ultimately about things that surpass the power of sight. Hidden in Jesus, and hidden in his church, is the gorgeous truth of a perfect reconciliation with God and our fellow human beings. It is that reconciliation which stands over and above all outward fights, fissures, and failures in the church.

On Sunday morning we show up in different congregations and denominations, but in the Father's eyes, we're all members of the same body of the same Son who claims us as brothers and sisters. We may see stains and blemishes in the church, but Jesus does not. He presents the church, his bride, to himself "in splendor, without spot or wrinkle or any such thing."[14]

That is the best of news. We are "without spot or wrinkle or any such thing." So is the grumpy old man at the end of the pew. So are the gossipy women gathered around the coffeepot after the service. So is the pastor, who spent the week wrestling with doubts and fatigue. We gather around a bath, a word, and a meal with the Savior who is in love with sinners. He loves and forgives us and bids us love and forgive one another.

In this community of the broken, the struggling, the weak, we learn that what it means to be a church is not to be perfect, but to be called the chosen of God.

CHAPTER NINE

Stewards of Our Scars

IN DARKNESS we began this journey together. We sat alongside our father, Adam, as he watched the western horizon swallow his source of light and warmth. A Jewish legend says he endured that first night mourning the loss of his precious sun because he knew nothing of sunrises. And he wasn't aware that his Father was the God of midnight as well as the Lord of noon. As I imagine it, during those lightless hours, God must have seemed ominously absent to Adam.

In darkness we will also end our journey together, but in a night wholly unlike our forefather's first night. These dark hours before dawn are charged with struggle. Two combatants brawl in the night on the banks of a river. One is man; one is God. In a Bible full of bizarre stories with bizarre endings, this one, perhaps more than any other narrative in Scripture, reveals what beats deep within the heart of God for us, his children.

The story tells us that Jacob was ending his own journey. He was finally coming home, though he was far from certain what kind of homecoming it would be. Twenty years had elapsed since he had lived up to (really, *down* to) his name: Jacob means "cheater, supplanter, over-reacher, heel-grabber." Not an endearing name. Then again, Jacob isn't exactly an endearing character. He's a conniving, plotting, life-revolves-around-me kind of character. Years before, rather than feeding his famished brother, he took advantage of Esau's hunger to barter for his birthright.[1] Later, Jacob took advantage of his aging father's blindness, repeatedly lying to Isaac while dressing in Esau's clothes. And while Esau was out hunting, Jacob poached the blessing reserved for Esau.[2] That's what lit the fuse of Esau's anger. When he realized his kid brother had cheated him out of his rightful inheritance, Esau vowed to kill him. Jacob escaped to his mother's kinfolk, out of reach of Esau's bloodlust. For two decades he remained in exile, until, finally, God told him it was time to go back home.

IT'S NOT ALWAYS EASY to come home. Many of us know that all too well, especially if we left under less-than-ideal circumstances. We have to look right in the eye those whom we have cheated—our own Esaus. Or, worse, we're afraid that people back home won't look *us* in the eye. They'll turn their backs. Home is not always where the heart is, after all; it is sometimes where the enemy is. In exile we lug around the baggage of our shame, guilt, and regret. It colors our perception of what the future will hold, what kind of homecoming it will be. We fear that perhaps we should have stayed in exile. Sometimes coming home brings home our worst fears.

When he was near home, Jacob dispatched servants ahead of him, who reported that his brother Esau was coming out to meet him. With four hundred men. Jacob assumed—reasonably—that his brother was on the warpath. If revenge is a dish best served cold, then Esau's dish had been perfectly cooled during those twenty long years. When he found out that his brother was heading his way, Jacob prepared for a clash, knowing he'd be no match for his older brother. Remembrance of his past cheating and conniving fueled his anxiety. As Jacob moved closer to his old home ground, he divided his family. He prayed. He escorted his wives and children across the Jabbok River. And then Jacob was left alone. Utterly alone. In the darkness. With his fears.

Alone, however, is sometimes where we need to be, where we must be. Sometimes the truth can only get to us when we're cut off from others. Without friends or coworkers to distract us. Without a spouse to comfort us. Without children tugging at our sleeves. It's the ideal time for God to work on us. Not like a mechanic works on a vehicle or an artist works on a painting. It feels more like God is working us over. Because he is.

THE LORD INVADED Jacob's loneliness in the form of an anonymous, human attacker. "A man wrestled with him," the Scriptures record.[3] At other times in the Old Testament, God appears temporarily in human form, but this encounter is unique. In Eden, God took a stroll. Meeting Abraham, God and his angelic compadres broke bread. But with Jacob, God steps into the ring for a knock-down, drag-out fight, man to man. For the patriarch Jacob, his usual tricks won't work—not conniving and usurping, not dressing up like his brother, not running away. The mask is off, as are the gloves. And the fight is on. All of Jacob vs. all of God.

All of us is exactly what God wants. We treat him like a visitor to our home, inviting him to sit on the sofa in the family room. We don't show him our unmade beds, open cluttered closets, or shine a flashlight under the fridge. But he refuses to be treated as a guest. He demands utter, complete ownership of us, so he wrestles us to the ground. Wrestling is a whole-body, whole-mind, whole-heart kind of sport. And God is in it to win us. We are "manhandled by God," as Gregory Schulz describes it.[4] He forces us to engage him with all of who we are—no compartmentalization allowed. In this struggle, all our preconceived notions about him fly out the window. Here is raw divinity. The Lord in our face. Rolling in the dirt with us, toe to toe. Alone with God, attacked by him, we have no other option than to fight.

Jacob wrestled with this man "until the breaking of the day."[5] Years before, Jacob had used the darkness of his father's eyes to his advantage. Blind Isaac couldn't see the son over whom he pronounced the blessing. Now the tables have been turned: it is Jacob whose vision is eclipsed. He's in the dark now. During the small hours of the night, the Lord looms large, filling those nocturnal hours with a violent love. Time ceases to be measured by seconds and minutes. Instead, it is counted by blows and falls and bruises in the night. And the fight will go on until the dawn of defeat or victory.

We all want to know how long our night of wrestling will last. When will I get my life back on track?

When will I finally feel better? When will the pain and regret go away? It's not surprising that the most frequent question asked by the Psalmist is, "How long, O LORD?" The answer is always the same: until the breaking of the day. Until the time when the Lord sees fit to usher in the dawn. Until he has used the darkness to his own advantage and—in ways unseen and often unfelt by us—to our own advantage.

During the fight, Jacob discovered part of who God is. "When the man saw that he did not prevail against Jacob, he touched his hip socket, and Jacob's hip was put out of joint as he wrestled with him."[6] God fights dirty. He doesn't play by the rules we've established. He doesn't respect our boundaries. He hits below the belt. Jacob won't strut away from this fight with the Lord; he will hobble away.[7] This battle will leave him a changed man in more ways than one. He will come out of the darkness as a man who walks in the light with a limp from God.

CHRISTIANITY HAS far too many voices that would have us believe in a God who doesn't wound us. But God himself declares otherwise: "See now that I, even I, am he, and there is no god beside me; I kill and I make alive; I wound and I heal."[8] God knows that it is only in our weakness and woundedness that we simultaneously discover our own ineptitude and his healing power. Without wounds we foster an image of ourselves as strong and healthy.

But the hands that wound us—they themselves bear the stigmata of grace. Our Savior kills, but only to make alive; wounds, but only to heal. He is conforming us to his cruciform likeness so that we see ourselves exclusively in his resurrection reflection. This is Christian growth: to become in our weakness more and more dependent on his strength, to seek in our woundedness more and more of his healing.

Like Jacob, we walk in the light with a limp from God. And that limp, far from a curse, is a constant reminder that we have been touched by our Savior.

In this fight, Jacob discovers more of God than the power of his wounding hand. The Lord blesses him with a new name—a name that encapsulates the mysterious, backwards love of God. As dawn approaches, Jacob's opponent says, "Let me go, for the day has broken."[9] But the patriarch refuses. "I will not let you go unless you bless me." The man asks, "What is your name?" When Jacob tells him, the Lord says, "Your name shall no longer be called Jacob, but Israel, for you have striven with God and with men, and have prevailed."[10] Israel means "he who fights with God."

But Jacob doesn't merely fight with God; he wins. The Lord loses. The Creator of heaven and earth is bested by one of his own creatures. This would be shocking even if the victor were the highest and holiest sage of impeccable character. But it's *Jacob*—heel-grabbing, lying, deceiving, conniving, thieving Jacob. A rank sinner prevails over the Almighty. When the fight is over, when the dust has settled, Israel comes out on top. And God, far from a sore loser, greatly rejoices in his own defeat.

JESUS TURNS all our assumptions about and expectations of God on their head. He meets us in the darkness of our own rebellion. We wrestle with him in a fight that we can't possibly win. And when light dawns, we discover the impossible has become not only possible but absolutely certain: Jesus has lost, and we are victorious. Jacob's eureka moment happened on the banks of the Jabbok River. Ours happens on the blood-soaked soil beneath the cross of Christ, where he is vanquished by us. Defeated by our death. Bested by our sin.

In that moment, we finally grasp how far our God was willing to go for us to win. He became last, that we might become first. He became servant of all to make us kings and queens. He became dead to make us alive.

Like Jacob, we have striven with God and with men—indeed, with God *as* man—yet have prevailed.

The joy of Jesus is the victory of those who have no chance to win. But we win on the cross because in our stead is the one who assumes our sin and death and rebellion—and gives us a new name. No longer shall we be called Sinners but Saints. No more shall we bear a label of shame; now we shall be crowned with the title of grace.

That, finally, is how Christ brings us home from exile. Whatever our story might be, however dark and sordid the details, at the core of our narrative is the God who will stop at nothing to bring us home to himself. The God who pursued humanity from heaven to earth, who entangled himself in the foul and twisted ways of a world gone mad, until finally he was swallowed by the grave—this God will pursue each of us. He will move heaven and earth to find us. There is no escaping the God who fills even the deepest, darkest cracks into which we fall.

THERE'S AN ODD LITTLE DETAIL at the close of the story of Jacob's wrestling match with the Lord. Jacob was "limping because of his hip." "Therefore," the text adds, "to this day the people of Israel do not eat the sinew of the thigh that is on the hip socket, because he touched the socket of Jacob's hip on the sinew of the thigh."[11] The sacred wound of Jacob was stamped onto the hips of every animal his descendants might consume. Keeping alive the memory of God's touch, and out of a reverent remembrance, they refrained from eating that particular part. For God's people, Jacob's limp was an ongoing handicap. By it they recalled the Lord who conceals his blessings in the wounds of his people. The one-time divine touch became a sacred, memorial scar.

Up and down the highways we travel are billboards that promise all our bodily imperfections can be erased with a few visits to the right physician. Bigger breasts and a well-rounded backside can be purchased. Botox can smooth out the wrinkles of time. Love handles can be shrunk to a mere pinch. Scars from acne or surgery can be erased from our skin. If our wallets are big enough, our bodies can be young enough, sexy enough, toned enough. The message preached by every advertisement is this: Only a fool would keep his or her imperfections. In our culture the new sin has become keeping our scars.

But some scars are not only too deep for the surgeon's knife; they're too important to be erased. These blemishes are storytellers. They keep alive memories that, while punctuated with pain and regret, are also full of grace and healing.

In the past, I often wondered why the books of the Bible are scarred. Inked onto those pages are the blemishes of men and women whose stories we met briefly in this book. Cain with his murder. Noah with his drunkenness. Jacob with his deceit. My friend Elmer was shocked when he read about Lot and his daughters. The failures of God's people often strike us that way. But as I came to realize, those scarred stories remain in the body of this sacred book because they are our Father's gifts to us. They warn us of the dangers we face on the path of life. They hold before us a mirror of our shared, human weaknesses. And most importantly, they disclose a God whose "anger is but for a moment, and [whose] favor is for a lifetime."[12] The last thing we need to lose is our scars: the gracious favor of God makes sacred these marks of our old sins.

YEARS AGO, while Frederick Buechner was speaking to a group of Christians at a Texas retreat, he recounted a painful incident from his childhood. Afterward, a man named Howard Butt approached him and said, "You have had a good deal of pain in your life, and you have been a good steward of it."[13] His words took Buechner aback. He had never thought of pain, and its impact on his life, in terms of stewardship. But the more he reflected on what it means to be a steward, the more he realized how true the man's words had been. Later, he wrote, "If you manage to put behind you the painful things that happen to you as if they never really happened or didn't really matter all that much when they did, then the deepest and most human things you have in you to become are not apt to happen either."[14]

Whatever sufferings we have endured, self-inflicted or otherwise, are scars our Father has granted us as a sacred duty. Stewards do not own that for which they are responsible; they are called to faithfully manage what another has given them. Our scars are God's gifts to us. They are the means Jesus uses not to anchor us to the past but to propel us into the future as those who know the wounding power and healing grace of God.

Buechner speaks of "the deepest and most human things you have in you to become." Chief among those is the capacity to reflect to those around us the love of God of which we have so deeply drunk. The most human thing we can do is to live in the image of the God of compassion who made us and remade us in his Son. We don't forget the scars of that remaking. We learn to treasure them as life-altering wounds that teach us what it means to be children of the heavenly Father.

Remember Paul's thorn in the flesh? The Lord refused to take it away, saying, "My grace is sufficient for you, for my power is made perfect in your weakness."[15] Paul then added, "Therefore, I will boast all the more gladly of my weaknesses, so that the power of Christ may rest upon me." So it is with our stewardship of scars.

The resurrected body of Jesus must be a magnificent sight. Glorious, radiant, perfect. Yet for me, the most precious aspects of Jesus's body are the scars that remain, even after Easter. The nail prints in his hands. The spear-pierced hole in his side. The gashes left by spikes in his feet. These everlasting wounds visually preach the gospel. As Isaiah prophesied, "With his stripes we are healed."[16]

Jesus is the steward of his own scars. He uses them to grant peace to his astonished disciples in the Upper Room.[17] With them he beckons Thomas out of his doubt.[18] And with these scars he continues not only to grant us peace, but to imbue our own scars with meaning and grace.

MY SCARS. Your scars. The scars of our Lord. They are, in truth, all one, for we are a body united by the Spirit.

Because Jesus has baptized us into himself, we are the body of Christ. Our stories all merge in the one story of a God who became one of us. He shares our flesh and blood. He took into himself our frailties, our sicknesses, our sins. He became as we are so that we might become as he is. So intimate is our union with Jesus, and one another, that our Father sees us as one person. In the eyes of God, we are all bound together in the crucified, resurrected body of Jesus.

That, finally, is where the long, crooked road of repentance leads us, where it always leads us: into Jesus, who has walked with us—indeed, carried us—every step along the way. On our darkest days on the darkest path, he was there. When we stumbled again, he was there. When we limp away from our fights with him, he is ever-present.

Look at your scars and cherish them. They are icons of divine love. They are transfigured by the grace of the God who will always call us by one name: Beloved.

Bibliography

Bonhoeffer, Dietrich. *Life Together*. New York: Harper & Row, 1954.

Brown, Steve. *Scandalous Freedom*. New York: Howard Books, 2004.

Buechner, Frederick. *Secrets in the Dark: A Life in Sermons*. New York: HarperCollins, 2006.

Capon, Robert Farrar. *Between Noon and Three: Romance, Law, and the Outrage of Grace*. Grand Rapids: Eerdmans, 1997.

————. *Kingdom, Grace, Judgment: Paradox, Outrage, and Vindication in the Parables of Jesus*. Grand Rapids: Eerdmans, 2002.

Crandall, Kimm. *Beloved Mess: God's Perfect Love for Your Imperfect Life*. Grand Rapids: Baker Books, 2016.

Davis, Heather Choate. *Man Turned in on Himself: Understanding Sin in 21st-Century America*. Icktank Press, 2014.

Evans, Rachel Held. *Searching for Sunday: Loving, Leaving, and Finding the Church*. Nashville: Nelson Books, 2015.

Fitzpatrick, Elyse. *Because He Loves Me: How Christ Transforms Our Daily Life*. Wheaton, IL: Crossway Books, 2008.

Forde, Gerhard. *On Being a Theologian of the Cross: Reflections on Luther's Heidelberg Disputation, 1518*. Grand Rapids: Eerdmans, 1997.

Hein, Steven A. *The Christian Life: Cross or Glory?* Irvine, CA: New Reformation Publications, 2015.

Keller, Timothy. *The Prodigal God: Recovering the Heart of the Christian Faith.* New York: Penguin Books, 2008.

Luther, Martin. *Luther's Works.* American Edition. 56 vols. St. Louis: Concordia Publishing House and Philadelphia: Fortress Press, 1955–1986.

Peterson, Eugene. *Under the Unpredictable Plant: An Exploration of Vocational Holiness.* Grand Rapids: Eerdmans, 1992.

Schulz, Gregory P. *The Problem of Suffering: A Father's Hope.* St. Louis: Concordia Publishing House, 2011.

Sprinkle, Preston. *Charis: God's Scandalous Grace for Us.* Colorado Springs: David C. Cook, 2014.

Swoboda, A. J. *A Glorious Dark: Finding Hope in the Tension between Belief and Experience.* Grand Rapids: Baker Books, 2014.

Thompson, Jessica. *Everyday Grace: Infusing All Your Relationships with the Love of Jesus.* Bloomington, MN: Bethany House Publishers, 2015.

Wright, N. T. *Simply Jesus: A New Vision of Who He Was, What He Did, and Why He Matters.* New York: HarperOne, 2011.

Yancey, Philip. *The Bible Jesus Read: Why the Old Testament Matters.* Grand Rapids: Zondervan, 2010.

Notes

Notes to the Foreword

1. Heidelberg-Catechism.com, sponsored by the Canadian Reformed Theological Seminary: http://www.heidelberg-catechism .com/en/lords-days/1.html.

2. Karl Barth, *Church Dogmatics, Volume IV: The Doctrine of Reconciliation, Part 1,* translated by G. W. Bromiley (London: T.& T. Clark, 1956), p. 104.

3. From Luther's Small Catechism, Concordia Publishing House: http://catechism.cph.org/en/lords-prayer.html.

4. Karl Barth, *Church Dogmatics, Volume IV: The Doctrine of Reconciliation, Part 1,* p. 251.

Notes to Chapter 1

1. Genesis 4, 9, 12, 14, 16, 19, 27, 29–30, 34, 35, 37, respectively.

2. Eccles. 1:9.

3. For an in-depth treatment of the meaning and origin of this phrase, along with its popular manifestations in modern life, see Heather Choate Davis, *Man Turned in on Himself: Understanding Sin in 21st-Century America* (Icktank Press, 2014).

Notes to Chapter 2

1. Gen. 3:5.
2. Gen. 3:7.
3. A. J. Swoboda, *A Glorious Dark: Finding Hope in the Tension between Belief and Experience* (Grand Rapids: Baker Books, 2014), p. 20.
4. Robert Farrar Capon, *Between Noon and Three: Romance, Law, and the Outrage of Grace* (Grand Rapids: Eerdmans, 1997), p. 145.
5. Exod. 6:9.
6. Exod. 14:12.
7. Num. 14:2-4.
8. Ps. 113:5-6.
9. Ps. 113:7.
10. Luke 1:48, 51-52.
11. Martin Luther, *The Sermon on the Mount (Sermons) and the Magnificat*, vol. 21 of *Luther's Works* (St. Louis: Concordia Publishing House, 1956), pp. 299-30. Emphasis mine.
12. Luther, *Magnificat*, p. 301.
13. Luther, *Magnificat*, p. 299.
14. Gerhard Forde, *On Being a Theologian of the Cross: Reflections on Luther's Heidelberg Disputation, 1518* (Grand Rapids: Eerdmans, 1997), pp. 112-13.
15. Martin Luther, "Heidelberg Disputation," in *Career of the Reformer: I*, vol. 31 of *Luther's Works* (Philadelphia: Fortress Press, 1957), p. 57.
16. Ps. 139:12.

Notes to Chapter 3

1. Philip Yancey, *The Bible Jesus Read: Why the Old Testament Matters* (Grand Rapids: Zondervan, 2010), p. 121.
2. Psalm 88, verses 6, 18, 6, 7, 8, and 17 respectively.
3. Ps. 44:9, 10, 14.
4. Ps. 60:3.
5. Ps. 74:1.
6. Ps. 80:5.
7. Ps. 89:38-39.

8. Ps. 10:1.

9. Ps. 13:1–2.

10. Ps. 74:1.

11. Ps. 77:7–9.

12. Deut. 29:29.

13. Ps. 22:1; Matt. 27:46; Mark 15:34.

14. Ps. 10:1.

15. Ps. 13:1–2.

16. Ps. 77:9.

17. Dietrich Bonhoeffer, *Life Together* (New York: Harper & Row, 1954), p. 46.

18. Bonhoeffer, *Life Together*, p. 45.

19. Ps. 88:1.

20. Ps. 44:10.

21. Ps. 89:38.

22. 2 Cor. 5:21.

23. Ps. 40:6; 40:12. In Hebrews 10:5–7, Christ is the one speaking Psalm 40:6.

24. Ps. 41:9; John 13:18; Ps. 41:4.

25. Isa. 53:2.

26. Ps. 13:1.

27. Heb. 4:15.

28. Jessica Thompson, *Everyday Grace: Infusing All Your Relationships with the Love of Jesus* (Bloomington, MN: Bethany House Publishers, 2015), p. 152.

29. Elyse Fitzpatrick, *Because He Loves Me: How Christ Transforms Our Daily Life* (Wheaton, IL: Crossway, 2008), p. 24.

Notes to Chapter 4

1. Luke 15:13.

2. Rom. 5:10.

3. Kimm Crandall, *Beloved Mess: God's Perfect Love for Your Imperfect Life* (Grand Rapids: Baker Books, 2016), p. 96.

4. Luke 23:34.

5. Luke 15:20.

6. Timothy Keller, *The Prodigal God: Recovering the Heart of the Christian Faith* (New York: Penguin Books, 2008), p. 24.

Notes to Chapter 5

1. Rom. 7:15.
2. Rom. 7:18.
3. Rom. 7:19.
4. Frederick Buechner, *Secrets in the Dark: A Life of Sermons* (New York: HarperCollins, 2006), p. 247.
5. Rom. 7:15.
6. Rom. 7:24.
7. Jer. 17:9.
8. John Calvin, *Institutes of the Christian Religion*, I.XI.8.
9. Rom. 7:24.

Notes to Chapter 6

1. Gen. 19:30-38.
2. 2 Pet. 2:7-8.
3. Gen. 13:5-13.
4. Gen. 13:13.
5. Gen. 19:8.
6. Gen. 19:16.
7. Kimm Crandall, *Beloved Mess: God's Perfect Love for Your Imperfect Life* (Grand Rapids: Baker Books, 2016), p. 44. Crandall's entire book is about living an unmasked life.
8. Steven Hein, *The Christian Life: Cross or Glory?* (Irvine, CA: New Reformation Publications, 2015), p. 41. Italics in original.
9. Rachel Held Evans, *Searching for Sunday: Loving, Leaving, and Finding the Church* (Nashville: Nelson Books, 2015), p. 70.
10. Dietrich Bonhoeffer, *Life Together* (New York: Harper & Row, 1954), p. 110.
11. 2 Cor. 12:1-5.
12. 2 Cor. 12:4.
13. 2 Cor. 12:7.

14. 2 Cor. 12:8.

15. 2 Cor. 12:9.

16. As theologian Preston Sprinkle writes in *Charis: God's Scandalous Grace for Us*, "[N]o mess, no failure, no broken marriage, no affair, no night with a prostitute can prevent God from using you — an image-bearing masterpiece, frail and flawed, forever loved" (Colorado Springs: David C. Cook, 2014), p. 62.

17. 2 Cor. 4:7.

18. 2 Cor. 12:10.

19. John 3:30.

Notes to Chapter 7

1. Ps. 122:1.

2. Martin Luther, *Selected Psalms I*, vol. 12 of *Luther's Works* (St. Louis: Concordia Publishing House, 1955), p. 370.

3. Luther, *Selected Psalms I*, p. 370.

4. Luther, *Selected Psalms I*, p. 370.

5. Luther, *Selected Psalms I*, p. 372.

6. Luke 15:17.

7. Luke 15:19.

8. Luke 15:22-24.

9. Rom. 2:4.

10. 2 Tim. 2:13.

11. Robert Farrar Capon, *Kingdom, Grace, Judgment: Paradox, Outrage, and Vindication in the Parables of Jesus* (Grand Rapids: Eerdmans, 2002), p. 297.

12. Rom. 5:1.

Notes to Chapter 8

1. Eugene Peterson, *Under the Unpredictable Plant: An Exploration of Vocational Holiness* (Grand Rapids: Eerdmans, 1992), p. 22.

2. Peterson, *Under the Unpredictable Plant*, p. 17.

3. Matt. 16:23; John 13:27.

4. Acts 2:42-47; 5:1-11.

5. Acts 6:1; 15:1–5.

6. 1 Cor. 1:10–12; Gal. 1:6–9; Col. 2:18.

7. 1 Cor. 5:1.

8. Rev. 2:4, 14–15, 20; 3:1, 16.

9. Rachel Held Evans, *Searching for Sunday: Loving, Leaving, and Finding the Church* (Nashville: Nelson Books, 2015), p. 67.

10. Steve Brown, *Scandalous Freedom* (New York: Howard Books, 2004), p. 113.

11. Rom. 6:4.

12. Luke 10:16.

13. N. T. Wright, *Simply Jesus: A New Vision of Who He Was, What He Did, and Why He Matters* (New York: HarperOne, 2011), p. 180.

14. Eph. 5:27.

Notes to Chapter 9

1. Gen. 25:29–34.

2. Gen. 27:1–29.

3. Gen. 32:24.

4. Gregory Schulz, *The Problem of Suffering: A Father's Hope* (St. Louis: Concordia Publishing House, 2011), Chapter 4.

5. Gen. 32:24.

6. Gen. 32:25.

7. Gen. 25:31.

8. Deut. 32:39.

9. Gen. 32:26.

10. Gen. 32:28.

11. Gen. 32:31–32.

12. Ps. 30:5.

13. Frederick Buechner, *Secrets in the Dark: A Life in Sermons* (New York: HarperCollins, 2006), pp. 210–11.

14. Buechner, *Secrets in the Dark*, p. 212.

15. 2 Cor. 12:9.

16. Isa. 53:5.

17. John 20:20.

18. John 20:27.